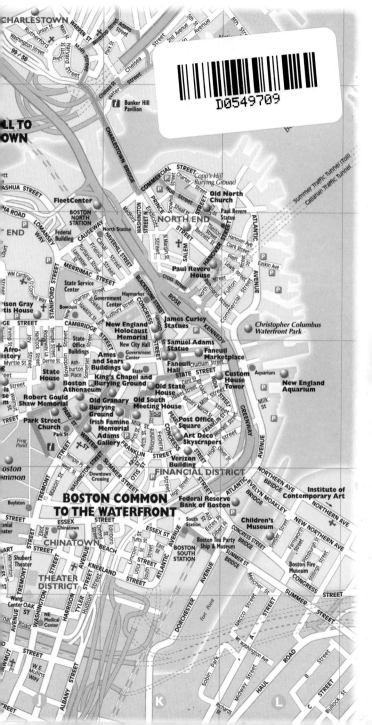

CHARLESTOWN

Rutherford

Union St

Washington Street

99 / 38

Winthrop Street

Warren Street

Adams Street

Main Street

Prescott

Park Street

Chelsea Street

2nd Avenue

Avenue

8th Street

Chelsea Street

Natter Street

Bunker Hill Pavilion

CHARLESTOWN BRIDGE

D0549709

Summer Traffic Tunnel (toll)

Callahan Traffic Tunnel

LL TO OWN

ASHUA STREET

HA ROAD

END

COMMERCIAL STREET

Charter Street

Copp's Hill Burying Ground

Hull Street

Snowhill Street

Old North Church

FleetCenter

BOSTON NORTH STATION

North Station

WASHINGTON

Endicott Street

PRINCE STREET

Salem Street

Sheafe Street

Bennett Street

Paul Revere Statue

Hanover Street

ATLANTIC

Federal Building

CAUSEWAY

HAVERHILL STREET

Canal Street

Friend Street

Portland Street

Lancaster Street

N. Margin Street

SALEM STREET

NORTH END

Hissou Street

Clark Street

Fleet Street

Lewis Street

Easkin Ave

AVENUE

LOMANSE WAY

WM Cardinal O'Connell Way

MERRIMAC STREET

BLACKSTONE STREET

Cross Street

Paul Revere House

North Bennett Street

Richmond Street

Commercial Street

Fulton Street

P

State Service Center

Charson Street

Hawkins St

Haymarket

ROSE

New Sudbury Street

CONGRESS STREET

KENNEDY

Christopher Columbus Waterfront Park

ison Gray tis House

GE STREET

STANFORD STREET

Bowdoin Street

CAMBRIDGE STREET

Government Center

New England Holocaust Memorial

James Curley Statues

Union Street

Afro-story

Myrtle St

Joy Street

Hancock Street

Temple Street

Irvine Place

Derne St

State Office Buildings

Somerset Street

New City Hall

Government Center

Ames and Sears Buildings

State

Samuel Adams Statue

Faneuil Marketplace

Chatham Street

Faneuil Hall

STATE STREET

Custom House Tower

Aquarium

New England Aquarium

eet

Is Street

State House

Ashburton Place

Bowdoin Street

King's Chapel and Burying Ground

Boston Athenaeum

State Street

Old State House

India Street

Central Street

Chatham Street

Broad Street

Water Street

Milk Street

P

Milk St

GREENWAY

TREET

Robert Gould Shaw Memorial

PARK STREET

Old Granary Burying Ground

Old South Meeting House

Province Street

Post Office Square

Franklin Street

Pearl Street

Oliver Street

High Street

Park Street Church

Park St

WINTER ST

Irish Famine Memorial

Adams Gallery

Arch St

FRANKLIN STREET

CONGRESS

Federal Street

Art Deco Skyscrapers

AVENUE

Frog Pond

oston mmon

Temple Pl

West St

Mason St

Downtown Crossing

SUMMER STREET

OTIS STREET

Verizon Building

FINANCIAL DISTRICT

High Street

Purchase Street

ATLANTIC

EVELYN MOAKLEY BRIDGE

NORTHERN AVE BRIDGE

Institute of Contemporary Art

NORTHERN AVE

Boylston

WASHINGTON STREET

TREMONT

BOSTON COMMON TO THE WATERFRONT

Federal Reserve Bank of Boston

South Station

Atlantic Ave

Children's Museum

NEW NORTHERN AVE

Fan Pier Street

Farnsworth Street

STREET

onial eater

Eliot Place

ESSEX STREET

Chinatown

ESSEX ST

Edinboro Street

Tufts St

ESSEX STREET

Essex Street

Gilbert St

CONGRESS STREET

Boston Tea Party Ship & Museum

SUMMER ST BRIDGE

Pittsburgh Street

Sleeper Street

Boston Fire Museum

CONGRESS

SUMMER

STREET

ART

Shubert Theater

Warrenton St

CHINATOWN

BEACH STREET

Lincoln Street

Utica Street

Kneeland St

BOSTON SOUTH STATION

ATLANTIC

AVENUE

Melcher St

STREET

THEATER DISTRICT

Tremont St

KNEELAND STREET

Dorchester Ave

Fort Point

Necco Street

M. Washington Ave

ROAD

STREET

Wang Center

OAK ST

HARRISON AVENUE

TYLER Street

Hudson Street

STREET

DORCHESTER AVENUE

Sobin Park

B Street

Street

AVENUE Road

NE Medical Center

WASHINGTON STREET

Midway Street

HAUL

C STREET

Bullock St

NUT STREET

W E Mullins Way

ALBANY STREET

Richards

REET

J

K

L

Boston's
25Best

by Sue Gordon

Fodor's Travel Publications
New York • Toronto •
London • Sydney • Auckland
www.fodors.com

How to Use This Book

KEY TO SYMBOLS

✚ Map reference to the accompanying fold-out map

✉ Address

☎ Telephone number

🕐 Opening/closing times

🍴 Restaurant or café

🚆 Nearest rail station

Ⓜ Nearest subway (Metro) station

🚌 Nearest bus route

⛴ Nearest riverboat or ferry stop

♿ Facilities for visitors with disabilities

❓ Other practical information

▷ Further information

ℹ Tourist information

✋ Admission charges: Expensive (over $10), Moderate ($6–$10), and Inexpensive ($5 or less)

⭐ Major Sight   ★ Minor Sight

👣 Walks   🚍 Excursions

🏬 Shops

🎵 Entertainment and Nightlife

🍴 Restaurants

This guide is divided into four sections

• Essential Boston: An introduction to the city and tips on making the most of your stay.
• Boston by Area: We've broken the city into five areas, and recommended the best sights, shops, entertainment venues, nightlife and restaurants in each one. Suggested walks help you to explore on foot.
• Where to Stay: The best hotels, whether you're looking for luxury, budget or something in between.
• Need to Know: The info you need to make your trip run smoothly, including getting about by public transportation, weather tips, emergency phone numbers and useful websites.

Navigation In the Boston by Area chapter, we've given each area its own color, which is also used on the locator maps throughout the book and the map on the inside front cover.

Maps The fold-out map accompanying this book is a comprehensive street plan of Boston. The grid on this fold-out map is the same as the grid on the locator maps within the book. We've given grid references within the book for each sight and listing.

Contents

Introducing Boston

From its 17th-century beginnings as a British colony, Boston has been a town of undeniable independent spirit. Its plucky revolutionaries earned it that reputation early on, and the city itself has upheld the tradition ever since.

Massachusetts has led many of the country's most important movements: public education, the abolition of slavery, women's equality and gay rights. Boston and Cambridge, its sister city across the Charles River (in this book, references to Boston include Cambridge), have been at the forefront of these campaigns.

The city's dedication to culture and learning is well known, and can be seen in its world-class museums, concert halls and libraries, and in the countless college campuses. Even the music clubs, galleries and movie theaters have their own histories.

Meanwhile, Boston's quality of life is equally high out of doors. The string of parks and public spaces designed by Frederick Law Olmsted (collectively known as the "Emerald Necklace") runs through the city, providing stunning and well-maintained green space in many a neighborhood. Water is almost always nearby or visible, from the Charles River Esplanade of Back Bay to the downtown area bordering Boston Harbor. And Boston's architecture is some of the most beautiful in the country: as often as not, Victorian brownstones share blocks with art deco buildings and contemporary skyscrapers.

Of course, none of these perks comes cheap. Boston's real estate is some of the most expensive in the country, and is seemingly ever on the rise. That's largely because, unlike many American cities, it has made urban living desirable, so its residents are willing to spend what's necessary. All in all, there are few cities in America more worth taking up residence in—or visiting.

Facts + Figures

- The "T" was the US's first subway system. The first section opened in 1897.
- Boston Common was the first public park in America.
- Harvard University was the first college in North America.

ODD FACTS

- Some 58 percent of Boston is built on landfill.
- There are more universities and colleges in Boston and Cambridge than anywhere else in the US.
- The Boston University Bridge is the only place in the world where a boat can sail under a train driving under a car driving under a plane.

LOCAL PASSIONS

● Ice cream (they eat more of it in Boston than any other city in the US).
● Baseball (traffic brings the area around Fenway Park to a halt for every game).
● Music (from local bands to symphony orchestras).

GETTING YOUR BEARINGS

Boston Common and the Public Garden lie at the heart of Boston. To their north is the old residential area of Beacon Hill. Southeast of the Common are the Theater District and Chinatown. The Freedom Trail, which starts on the Common, runs northeast through Old Boston, past Faneuil Hall to the Italian North End. Across the Charles River lies Harvard Square in Cambridge.

A Short Stay in Boston

DAY 1

Morning Arrive at the parking lot of the **New England Aquarium** (▷53) at 8.30 and duck into the restaurant **Sel de la Terre** (▷62) for its selection of fresh-baked breads, croissants and coffee. When the Aquarium opens at 9, walk its corridors to see both exotic and local sealife.

Mid-morning Make your way to **Faneuil Hall and Marketplace** (▷26) perusing the artist carts and watching the street performers along the way. Then walk past City Hall on to Tremont Street, and take a right on Beacon Street for a walk over historic **Beacon Hill** (▷24–25). After admiring the gold-domed **State House** (▷35), pass behind it down Mount Vernon Street, and take in posh **Louisburg Square** (▷24–25) and quaint, cobbled Acorn Street.

Lunch At the bottom of the hill, take a right on **Charles Street** (▷42). Stop at **Artù** (▷45) at 89 Charles Street for a panini, salad or pizza.

Afternoon Visit the antiques shops on Charles Street or visit **Nichols House** (▷39) or the **Museum of Afro-American History** (▷39).

Mid-afternoon Continue to the end of Charles Street, past the T station to the **Liberty Hotel** (▷112) for a drink in the Clink bar, and to admire the stunning architectural transformation of this former city jail.

Dinner Return to Charles Street for dinner at the **Beacon Hill Bistro** (▷45) or at the nearby **Upper Crust Pizzeria** (▷46) for authentic Italian pizzas.

Evening Take a 10-minute walk through **Boston Common** or the **Public Garden** (▷50–51), or a five-minute taxi ride around it, to the Theater District, to see a play in any of the city's excellent theaters.

DAY 2

Morning Start the day with a Parisian or American breakfast at **Brasserie JO** (▷ 84), opposite the Prudential Center, and continue along Huntington Avenue past Symphony Hall to the **Museum of Fine Arts** (▷ 70). It's easy to spend a day among its vast collections of French Impressionists, Egyptian artifacts and Early American decorative arts.

Mid-morning Walk along the Fens to the **Isabella Stewart Gardner Museum** (▷ 68–69) for a look at the home of a Boston legend and a stroll through her fabulous art collection.

Lunch Take the T to Harvard Square for lunch at **Z Square** (▷ 98), a few steps from the station. Order takeout for a picnic beside the Charles River, or rest your weary feet by dining in the smart restaurant downstairs.

Afternoon Cross Harvard Yard to see the one-of-a-kind collection of glass flowers at the **Harvard Museum of Natural History** and a look at the Native American collections at the adjoining **Peabody Museum** (▷ 89).

Mid-afternoon Take a break from museums at **L. A. Burdick Chocolate** café (▷ 98) before continuing down Brattle Street for a look at the **Longfellow House** (▷ 92).

Dinner Continue down Tory Row and through the tree-lined streets of elegant homes to dinner at **Craigie Street Bistro** (▷ 98), where the "Chef's Whim menu" features a multicourse dinner at a reasonable price. Or dine right in the Square at **Sandrine's** (▷ 98), where you can enjoy the Alsatian chef/owner's blend of French styles and seasonal local ingredients.

Top 25

▶ ▶ ▶

Beacon Hill and Louisburg Square ▷ 24–25
Elegant residential district with some historic homes.

USS *Constitution* and Charlestown ▷ 36–37
Naval museums and historic warships.

Trinity Church and Copley Square ▷ 76–77
New (John Hancock Tower) and old (Trinity Church) architecture rub shoulders in this square.

State House ▷ 35
The gold-domed landmark center of state government.

The South End ▷ 74–75
Lively, sought-after residential area with excellent restaurants and shops.

Prudential Center and Skywalk ▷ 73 An upscale shopping mall and stunning panoramic views from the 50th floor.

Paul Revere House ▷ 34 The legendary revolutionary's North End home and one of the few houses left from colonial America.

Boston Athenaeum ▷ 51 A Boston institution, haunt of intellectuals and the country's first library.

Boston Common and Public Garden ▷ 50 Open-air playgrounds, ponds and gardens.

Old State House ▷ 30–31 Best museum for an overview of Boston's rich history.

North End and the Old North Church ▷ 32–33 Historic church in the heart of Little Italy.

New England Aquarium ▷ 53 A large collection—families will love this. Don't miss feeding time.

These pages are a quick guide to the Top 25, which are described in more detail later. Here they are listed alphabetically, and the tinted background shows which area they are in.

Boston Harbor Islands
▷ **102** Unspoiled havens of wildlife, historic forts and beaches.

Boston Public Library
▷ **66** Marbles, mosaics and murals in an oasis of tranquillity.

Commonwealth Avenue
▷ **67** Boston's grandest houses flank a green mall with noted statues.

Faneuil Hall and Marketplace ▷ **26** From first public meeting hall to food market and mall.

Harrison Gray Otis House ▷ **27** Restored Federal-style family home.

Harvard University Museums ▷ **88–89** Four world-quality museums.

Harvard Square and Harvard University
▷ **90–91** Cafés, shops, street entertainers—the hub of student life.

Institute of Contemporary Art ▷ **52** Cutting-edge architecture on the waterfront.

Isabella Stewart Gardner Museum ▷ **68–69** Superb works of art displayed in a palazzo setting.

JFK Library and Museum ▷ **103** Insight into JFK's life. His papers are held here.

BEACON HILL TO
CHARLESTOWN
20–46

Bunker Hill
Monument

CHARLESTOWN

National
Historical
Park

USS
Constitution

Museum
of Science

Charles
River Dam

Old North
Church

EAST
CAMBRIDGE

WEST END

NORTH
END

Charlesbank
Park

Paul Revere
House

Christopher
Columbus
Waterfront Park

Harrison Gray
Otis House

State
House

Faneuil
Marketplace

BEACON
HILL

Louisburg
Square

Esplanade

Boston
Athenaeum

Faneuil
Hall

Boston
Common

Old State
House

FINANCIAL
DISTRICT

New England
Aquarium

Boston
Harbor
Islands

Boston
Inner
Harbor

Public
Garden

Commonwealth
Avenue

Prudential
Center

Trinity Church
and Copley Square

CHINATOWN

THEATER
DISTRICT

BOSTON COMMON
TO THE WATERFRONT
47–62

Institute of
Contemporary Art

Boston
Public Library

Prudential
Skywalk

SOUTH
END

BACK BAY AND
THE SOUTH END
63–84

SOUTH
BOSTON

John F Kennedy
Library and Museum

Newbury Street ▷ **72** Funky shops, luxury boutiques, pavement cafés and trendy restaurants.

Museum of Science ▷ **28–29** Cutting-edge exhibits cover ocean waves to space travel.

Museum of Fine Arts ▷ **70–71** An exhaustive collection of treasures from around the globe.

Shopping

Some of Boston's best shopping areas are in the city's most attractive neighborhoods. One-of-a-kind shops selling clothes, books or antiques rub shoulders with outlets for contemporary crafts, innovative gifts and home accessories. Newbury Street is a joy, with its boutiques in lovely 19th-century brownstone buildings. People travel long distances to shop for clothes here, from top designer labels to the fabulously funky and the "gently used." With the great outdoors on the doorstep, many shops specialize in outdoors equipment and clothing.

Antiques

Like all of New England, Boston is good hunting ground for antiques. Clustered in and around Charles Street, at the foot of Beacon Hill, are dozens of shops. Most are specialists, selling oriental rugs, furniture, porcelain, silver or antique maps for serious money. Even if you can't afford to buy, it's a pleasure to browse. In Cambridge, hundreds of dealers in two large markets offer less expensive collectibles, alongside furniture, silverware and other antiques.

Books

Boston has a plethora of bookshops—new, used and antiquarian—particularly around Harvard Square. Whether you're looking for a coffee-table book on Boston to take back home, or something rare and erudite, you can browse undisturbed until 11pm in some stores.

ONLY IN BOSTON

Baked beans were invented in Boston by early colonists, who cooked them in molasses. Today, red Boston beans (albeit in candy form) are sold on souvenir stands. The lobster shows up in the usual touristy guises, from fridge magnets to pencil tops and notebooks. As for T-shirts, sweatshirts and baseball caps, they bear logos of local universities, like Harvard, and local teams, including the Patriots, the Bruins, the Celtics and, of course, 2004 and 2007 World Series winners, the Red Sox.

Downtown Crossing (top); painted shop sign (above middle); fishing flies for sale (middle)

Boutiques

Many of the small independent stores in Back Bay, Beacon Hill, the South End and Cambridge brim with interesting finds—from pottery made by Boston artists and soaps made by local beauty companies to hand-knit sweaters. Even on Newbury Street, which at first glance seems to be full of pricey international brands, you'll find local businesses tucked in among the heavy hitters.

Outlet Shopping

Some of New England's big outlets— where clothes, shoes and household goods are available at discounts of up to 65 percent—are within an hour of central Boston. They make a tempting day trip if you get a buzz from finding a bargain.

Farmers' Markets

At the farmers' markets that start up in spring in Copley Square (Tuesday, Friday), South Station (daily) and Harvard Square (Friday, Sunday), you can find all the goodies available at road-side farm stands around rural areas of New England—fresh fruits, ice cream, maple syrup, cheese and honey, among other things. Maple-cream candy (sweets) and plastic jugs of maple syrup make easy-to-pack souvenirs and gifts.

Contemporary Crafts

The best (and easy-to-find) places to shop for contemporary crafts are in Newbury and Charles streets, as well as in Cambridge and the South End.

Colorful handmade glass (top); shop sign (above middle); Faneuil Hall Marketplace (above)

UK TRAVELERS

If you are hunting for a bargain you should look in the malls and chain stores all over Boston, where clothes (except for woolens), leather goods and shoes are less expensive than back home. You will also find CDs at good prices.

Before you let your spending run wild, check the current customs limits for bringing goods back to the UK.

Shopping by Theme

You'll find all sorts of shops in Boston. On this page they are listed by theme with cross references to more detailed information.

ANTIQUES

Cambridge Antique Market (▷ 94)
Charles Street (▷ 42)
Danish Country Antiques (▷ 41)

BOOKS AND MAPS

Brattle Bookshop (▷ 58)
Curious George Goes to WordsWorth (▷ 95)
Grolier Poetry Bookshop (▷ 95)
Harvard Bookstore (▷ 94)
Harvard Coop (▷ 94)
Rand McNally (▷ 42)

FOR CHILDREN

Build-A-Bear (▷ 41)
Calliope (▷ 94)
Curious George Goes to WordsWorth (▷ 95)
Harvard Coop (▷ 94)
The Red Wagon (▷ 42)
Stellabella Toys (▷ 95)

CLOTHES

Alan Bilzerain (▷ 80)
Emporio Armani (▷ 80)
Filene's Basement (▷ 80)
Grettaluxe (▷ 80)
Holiday Boutique (▷ 42)
Jasmine Sola and Sola Men (▷ 95)
Linens on the Hill (▷ 42)
Louis Boston (▷ 58)
Marc Jacobs (▷ 80)
Nomad (▷ 95)

St. John Boutique (▷ 58)
Second Time Around (▷ 81)
Tess (▷ 95)
Urban Outfitters (▷ 95)
Via Vai (▷ 95)
Wish Boutique (▷ 42)

CRAFTS

Artful Hand (▷ 80)
Beadworks (▷ 94)
Cambridge Artists' Cooperative (▷ 94)
Charles Street (▷ 42)

DISTRICTS AND MALLS

Barneys New York (▷ 80)
CambridgeSide Galleria (▷ 41)
Downtown Crossing (▷ 58)
Faneuil Hall and Marketplace (▷ 27)
Harvard Square (▷ 94)
Newbury Street (▷ 81)
Prudential Center (▷ 81)

FOODS

Cardullo's (▷ 94)
Savenor's (▷ 42)

GIFTS/HOUSEHOLD

Abodeon (▷ 94)
Black Ink (▷ 41)
Boston Historical Society Museum Shop (▷ 41)
Boston Pewter Company (▷ 41)
Bromfield Pen Shop (▷ 58)
Copley Flair (▷ 80)

Crate & Barrell (▷ 41)
Eugene Galleries (▷ 41)
Flat of the Hill (▷ 42)
Four Preppy Paws (▷ 41)
Good, Inc (▷ 42)
The ICA Store (▷ 58)
Koo de Kir (▷ 42)
Lekker (▷ 80)
Matsu (▷ 81)
MDF (▷ 95)
Nostalgia Factory (▷ 42)
Pierre Deux (▷ 81)
Pottery Barn (▷ 81)
Simon Pearce (▷ 82)
Williams-Sonoma (▷ 81)

MUSIC

Newbury Comics (▷ 81)
Virgin Megastore (▷ 81)

OUTDOOR GEAR

Allen Edmonds (▷ 80)
Coach (▷ 41)
Dakini (▷ 94)
Foot Paths (▷ 58)
Hilton's Tent City (▷ 42)
Niketown (▷ 81)
The Rockport Store (▷ 81)
Skechers (▷ 58)
Tannery (▷ 58)

Boston by Night

The city that never sleeps, Boston's not. Even so, you'll find evening diversions aplenty.

Illuminations
For magical views of Boston's skyline visit the Prudential Skywalk, or cross over the Charles River to Cambridge on the T. Memorial Drive, between Longfellow and Harvard bridges, is a good spot to view the floodlit downtown sky-scrapers. In winter, trees twinkle with lights.

People-Watching
One of the liveliest spots for people-watching is the North End, where Italian music fills the narrow streets and restaurants hum with the chatter of Italian families. On Newbury Street people sit outdoors in cafés surveying the pedestrian parade.

Clubs and Bars
Boston club kids head for Lansdowne Street, near Kenmore Square. For cocktails and to catch the latest music, young professionals go to Boylston Place, a little alley in the Theater District. The RegattaBar (▷ 96) on Harvard Square is one of the best-known jazz venues in the east.

Late-Night Restaurants
Most restaurants do not serve after 10pm, but you could try Chinatown, where many places stay open until 4am. In the South End, several restaurants serve until 1am on weekends.

From top: Faneuil Hall; Fenway Park; view from the Prudential Tower; nightclub; Hatch Shell

LIVE ENTERTAINMENT

Entertaiment ranges from the Boston Symphony, Boston Ballet and traveling Broadway shows to rock concerts, avant-garde dance, and student theater. In summer, see free movies, concerts and theater on outdoor stages. There are summer concerts at Hatch Shell (▷ 82), as well as free movies. Watch for free band concerts on City Hall Plaza (☎ 617/635-4505) in July and August, and for performances by Boston Landmarks Orchestra (☎ 617/520-2200; www.landmarksorchestra. org).

Eating Out

Once known primarily as the home of beans and cod, Boston has blossomed into a first-rate culinary center.

Eclectic Menus
Where fried seafood and traditional Yankee fare once dominated menus, they're now offered alongside local seafood, with ceviche and mignonette-splashed oysters appearing regularly. Boston's restaurants are some of the country's best, from the snazzy bar-restaurants of Back Bay to its four-star New American ones.

Bistros
In general, bistros are the most popular genre of restaurant around town; they tend to show up as hip, candlelit spots on Newbury Street or family-run joints in the South End. What they have in common is a sophisticated but unpretentious quality, and often excellent food.

Elegant Dining
A level or two up in price and service, you'll find sophisticated dishes made by Boston's most admired chefs, many of whom have been in the city for years.

Ethnic Restaurants
Boston's ethnic cuisines go beyond Chinatown and the North End Italian neighborhood. In Cambridge, the Portuguese enclave is around Inman Square, and several Irish pubs are nearby. Elsewhere in the city are Ethiopian, Asian and Latin American restaurants.

OPENING TIMES

Restaurant times vary slightly all over the city, but most open for dinner between 5 and 6pm and a few serve dinner until 11pm or midnight, and offer an abridged menu if they happen to house a bar. Many of the trendier restaurants do not serve breakfast or lunch, and some are not open at all on Monday. Reservations are a must at any but the most casual places, but particularly for popular eating destinations like Back Bay and the South End.

From top: Newbury Street café; Faneuil Hall Marketplace; outdoor dining; Chinatown

Restaurants by Cuisine

There are restaurants to suit all tastes and budgets in Boston. On this page they are listed by cuisine. For a more detailed description of each restaurant, see Boston by Area.

AMERICAN AND MEXICAN

Brother Jimmy's (▷ 97)
Grill 23 & Bar (▷ 61)
Hungry I (▷ 45)
Icarus (▷ 84)
Plaza III, The Kansas City Steakhouse (▷ 46)
Slugger's Dugout (▷ 46)
Union Bar & Grille (▷ 84)

ASIAN AND MIDDLE EASTERN

Bombay Club (▷ 97)
Ginza (▷ 61)
Lala Rokh (▷ 45)
New Shanghai (▷ 62)
Sultan's Kitchen (▷ 46)

BOSTON'S BEST

Aujourd'hui (▷ 61)
Chez Henri (▷ 97)
Clio (▷ 84)
Durgin Park (▷ 45)
L'Espalier (▷ 84)
Excelsior (▷ 61)
Hamersley's Bistro (▷ 84)
No. 9 Park (▷ 46)
Om (▷ 98)
Radius (▷ 62)
Union Oyster House (▷ 46)
Upstairs on the Square (▷ 98)

BRUNCH

Sel de la Terrre (▷ 62)
Henrietta's Table (▷ 98)

COFFEE AND SNACKS

Caffè Paradiso (▷ 97)
Caffè Vittoria (▷ 45)
Flour Bakery (▷ 84)
Hi-Rise Bread Company (▷ 98)
Intrigue Café (▷ 61)
L. A. Burdick Chocolate (▷ 98)

ITALIAN AND MEDITERRANEAN

Antico Forno (▷ 45)
Artù (▷ 45)
Beacon Hill Bistro (▷ 45)
Cantina Italiana (▷ 45)
Mamma Maria (▷ 46)
Prezza (▷ 46)
Rialto (▷ 98)
Teatro (▷ 62)
Upper Crust Pizzeria (▷ 46)
Via Matta (▷ 62)

LATE EVENING

Barking Crab (▷ 61)
Bomboa (▷ 84)

SEAFOOD

Jumbo Seafood (▷ 62)
Kingfish Hall (▷ 45)
Legal Sea Foods (▷ 98)
Legal Test Kitchen (▷ 62)
Union Oyster House (46)

VEGETARIAN

Buddha's Delight (▷ 62)
Casablanca (▷ 97)
Milk Street Café (▷ 62)

If You Like...

However you'd like to spend your time in Boston, these top suggestions should help you tailor your ideal visit. Each sight or listing has a fuller write-up in Boston by Area.

LAZY MORNINGS

Take a stroll through the Public Garden (▷ 50).
Sip a coffee and people-watch from a table in Napoli Pastry (▷ 46) in the North End.
Walk along the Charles River Esplanade, the scenic pathway stretching along the river (▷ 78).
Go whale-watching out of Boston Harbor from the Aquarium (▷ 53).

SPECIALIST SHOPPING

Find the perfect shirt at a Newbury Street boutique (▷ 72).
Dig into some of the city's hottest music at Newbury Comics (▷ 81).
Act wonderfully childish at Curious George Goes to WordsWorth children's bookstore (▷ 94). Find one-of-a-kind crafts and handmade jewelry at the ICA Store (▷ 58). Discover new specialty cheeses and meats at Savenor's Market (▷ 42).

The swan boats in Boston Public Garden and trees on Charles River Esplanade (above)

BOSTON CULTURE

At Isabella Stewart Gardner Museum (▷ 68) see the stunning collection of international art in an attractive mansion.
View world-class collections at the Museum of Fine Arts (▷ 70): European and American art; Egyptian, Chinese and Classical artifacts.
Visit Trinity Church (▷ 76): A beautiful church founded before the Revolution.
Listen to the renowned Boston Symphony Orchestra at Symphony Hall (▷ 83).

The neo-Romanesque Trinity Church reflected in the I. M. Pei-designed John Hancock Tower (above right) and Boston Symphony Orchestra performing in the Symphony Hall (right)

Spectacular view of Boston at night (below)

SKYSCRAPERS

Explore Prudential Tower (▷ 73):
Shops, restaurants and souvenirs.
Admire the John Hancock Tower
(▷ 77): I. M. Pei & Partners designed
this glass-enclosed building, which
reflects the buildings surrounding it.
Ascend Custom House Tower
(▷ 38) for the great views from this
skyscraper-turned-hotel.

COMMUNING WITH NATURE

Relax in the Public Garden (▷ 50).
Manicured and bustling, it's filled with
citydwellers and tourists alike.
Amble through Back Bay Fens (▷ 78):
a string of parks, once a shallow bay.
Watch the boats go by in Christopher
Columbus Waterfront Park (▷ 38).
Experience the 265 acres (106ha) of lilac
blooms, roses and rare Asian trees at Arnold
Arboretum (▷ 104) in Cambridge.

A STATUE TRAIL

White swan in the Public Garden (above middle) and Arnold Arboretum (above)

See a dramatic ode to the first all-black
regiment to fight in the Civil War (▷ 56): Robert
Gould Shaw Memorial in Boston Common.
Make Way for the Ducklings: A charming
tribute to Robert McCloskey's children's book,
located in the Public Garden
(▷ 50).
Honor three women who
contributed to Boston's
history—Abigail Adams, Lucy
Stone, and Phillis Wheatley at
the Boston Women's Memorial
on Commonwealth Avenue
(▷ 67).

*Bronze statue in the Public Garden
(left), part of the collection inspired by
Robert McCloskey's children's story
"Make Way for the Ducklings"*

KEEPING THE CHILDREN OCCUPIED

Enjoy a fun, hands-on day of learning at the Museum of Science (▷ 28).
Find interactive exhibits on bubble-making, how televisions work and more at the Children's Museum (▷ 54).
Take a dramatic, spiral trip around a glowing tank full of sea creatures at the New England Aquarium (▷ 53).

The Children's Museum (below) and the Museum of Fine Arts (below middle)

BEING ENTERTAINED

Get in on the act: American Repertory Theatre (▷ 96) is Harvard's innovative and ambitious production house.
Watch a highly regarded company performing classical and contemporary productions at the Ballet Theatre of Boston (▷ 96).

LOOKING FOR A BARGAIN

Visit Harvard's three art museums (The Sackler, Fogg and Busch-Reisinger ▷ 89) free of charge on Saturday morning until noon.
At the Museum of Fine Arts, pay what you like for entry on Wednesday nights after 4pm (▷ 70).
Find half-price theater tickets the day of a performance at BosTix booths (▷ 59) at Faneuil Hall Marketplace and Copley Square.

The 18th-century Faneuil Hall (above)

ENJOYING NEW ENGLAND SEAFOOD

Head to Legal Sea Foods, (▷ 98) a local chain known for fresh lobsters and clam chowder.
Be more daring and head for Legal Test Kitchen (▷ 62) for international takes on the freshest seafood.

Delicious Pacific shrimp (right)

Boston by Area

This neighborhood merges historic buildings and monuments with skyscrapers.

SHEAFE STREET

Lexington Street
Prospect St
Vernon Street
Chestnut Street
Decatur Street
FATHER ADAMSKI MEMORIAL HIGHWAY
Adams Street
Chelsea Street
2nd Avenue
3rd Avenue
5th St
4th St
8th Street
Lincoln Avenue

National Historical Park

Constitution Museum

Shipyard House

Old Ironside

USS Constitution

Bunker Hill Pavilion

Boston Inner Harbor

Summer Traffic Tunnel (Toll)
Callahan Traffic Tunnel

COMMERCIAL STREET
BRIDGE
Charter Street
Hull Street
Snowhill Street
Copp's Hill Burying Ground
PRINCE STREET
WASHINGTON STREET N
ENDICOTT STREET
Medford
Sheaf St
Old North Church
Unity St
Paul Revere Statue
NORTH END
SALEM STREET
N Margin St
Tileston St
Bennett St
Hanover Ave
Clark street
HANOVER STREET
ATLANTIC AVENUE
Fleet St
North St
Lewis Street
Paul Revere House
Cross street
Richmond Street
Fulton
Commercial Street
Easkin Ave

ROSE STREET
BLACKSTONE STREET
KENNEDY
CONGRESS STREET
Union St
Haymarket Street
New England Holocaust Memorial
James Curley Statues
GREENWAY
Christopher Columbus Waterfront Park
New City Hall
Samuel Adams Statue
Faneuil Marketplace
Government Center State
Faneuil Hall
Chatham Street
Ames and Sears Buildings
STATE STREET
Custom House Tower
INDIA STREET
Old State House
Cent St

0   250 m
0   250 yds

K   L

Beacon Hill to Charlestown

Beacon Hill and Louisburg Square

DE LUCA'S MARKET

"FRESHEST BY FAR SINCE 1905"

HIGHLIGHTS

● Louisburg Square
● Pinckney Street and its view of Charles River
● Nichols House Museum
● Charles Street shops and restaurants

BOSTON BRAHMINS

● Oliver Wendell Holmes called those Bostonians who could trace their origins to the wealthy merchants of the 18th and 19th centuries, Brahmins after the high-ranking Hindu caste.

Beacon Hill is an enclave of elegant redbrick houses in a leafy maze of steep streets and narrow, cobbled lanes—it is a delightful area to explore on foot.

Brahmin stronghold After the opening of the State House on its southern slope, Beacon Hill was developed as a prestigious residential area by entrepreneurs including Boston's famous architect Charles Bulfinch. Boston's top families swiftly moved in. Rich as they were, these "Brahmins" were also the personification of Puritan reserve. Showiness was taboo, so the houses were restrained, with elegant doorways and ironwork gracing plain brick facades.

Perfectly preserved To get the magic of it all, choose a sunny day and just wander, noting the

Clockwise from left: Mount Vernon; leafy Louisburg Square; cobbled Acorn Street on Beacon Hill; a redbrick building in the Beacon Hill District; a mature tree in autumn in Beacon Hill; De Luca's Market on Charles Street

pillared porticoes, genteel fanlights and flowery window boxes. A walk through Beacon Hill leads you to some of the city's most treasured corners, including Mount Vernon Street, Chestnut Street, tiny Acorn Street and, best of all, Louisburg Square. Here Bulfinch's lovely bow fronts look onto a central garden reminiscent of a European square. Notice how the street lamps are lighted all day and look for the purple window panes: Manganese oxide in a batch of glass reacted with sunlight to produce discolored but now highly prized and very distinctive panes. To see inside a Beacon Hill home, visit the Nichols House Museum. On the hill's north slope from Pinckney Street down to Cambridge Street, the houses are smaller and more varied. It has several important sites in the history of Boston's African-American community, including the African Meeting House.

THE BASICS

⊞ H5

✉ Bounded by Beacon Street, Embankment Road, Cambridge Street, Bowdoin Street

🍴 Choice in Charles Street

Ⓟ Park Street, Charles/MGH, Arlington, Bowdoin (closed Sat)

♿ Steep hills, some uneven surfaces

❓ SPNEA tours of Beacon Hill, Black Heritage Trail: See Museum of Afro-American History (▷ 39)

Faneuil Hall and Marketplace

TOP 25

Market stand (below); a statue and avenue of trees lead to Faneuil Hall (right)

THE BASICS

www.faneuilhallmarket
place.com

🗺 K5

✉ Congress Street

☎ 617/242-5642

🕐 Great Hall: 9–5
(when not in use)

🍴 A plethora of eating
places

🚇 State, Aquarium,
Government Center

♿ Good

✋ Great Hall: free

❓ Great Hall: 15-min talk
every half-hour

HIGHLIGHTS

● Bulfinch meeting room
● Grasshopper weathervane
on the roof
● Quincy's granite market
buildings
● Street entertainers
● Food vendors in Quincy
Market

Faneuil Hall is a landmark for all Americans, the place where the iniquities of the British government were first debated in the 1770s. Now, its marketplace is a landmark for visitors.

"Cradle of Liberty" A wealthy trader of Huguenot origins, Peter Faneuil, presented the town with a market hall with a meeting room above. Ever since, the lower hall has been a market, and the galleried upper hall has been a place for public gatherings. In the 1700s, because the town meetings frequently discussed the problems with Britain that led up to the revolution and independence, Faneuil Hall became known as America's "Cradle of Liberty." Since then national issues, from the abolition of slavery to the Vietnam War, have been aired here. The room bears all the trademarks of Charles Bulfinch, the architect who built so much of Boston. He expanded the hall in 1805.

Quincy's marketplace Despite the Bulfinch expansion, more space was soon needed. In 1826, with some inspired town planning that radically changed Boston's waterfront, mayor Josiah Quincy filled in Town Dock and built over the wharves, providing a granite market hall flanked by granite warehouses. These were a wholesale food market until the 1960s. In the 1970s the area was renovated and revitalized, and is now the city's main tourist attraction (known as either Faneuil Hall Marketplace or Quincy Market) with dozens of shops, pushcarts, stands, eating places and street entertainers.

The elegant dining room (left) of Harrison Gray Otis House (below)

Harrison Gray Otis House

BEACON HILL TO CHARLESTOWN

★

TOP 25

This is Boston's only remaining Federal-style mansion. Meticulously restored in its every detail, the gracious interior is an accurate representation of how the upper classes lived in the 19th century.

Otis and Bulfinch One of the leading lights in post-Revolutionary Boston politics was the lawyer Harrison Gray Otis (1765–1844), long-standing friend of architect Charles Bulfinch. In 1796 he commissioned Bulfinch to build him this grand mansion in what was then the elegant area of Bowdoin Square. The structure's very restrained, very proper, brick facade is typical of what became known as the Federal style. Five years later, Bulfinch built Otis an even bigger house on newly developed Beacon Hill (▷ 24–25), to which all the wealthy were migrating. By the 1830s the Otis home had become a boarding house.

Authenticity In 1916 the Society for the Preservation of New England Antiquities bought the property as its headquarters. Accuracy and authenticity being its hallmarks, the SPNEA has restored the interior with reproduction wallpapers and paint colors (some surprisingly bright) based on paint analysis. Otis and his wife, Sally, were lavish entertainers and the parlor, dining room and drawing room, furnished in high Federal style, provide an insight into social manners of the day, while bedrooms, kitchens and servant quarters give you a glimpse of family life. One upstairs room shows the mansion as it looked when it was a boarding house.

THE BASICS

www.spnea.org
🔹 J4
✉ 141 Cambridge Street
☎ 617/227-3956
🕐 Wed–Sun 11–4.30. Tours on the hour and half hour
🍴 None
Ⓜ Bowdoin (closed Sat), Charles/MGH, Government Center
♿ Wheelchairs first floor only
💲 Moderate
SPNEA members free
❓ Walking tours of Beacon Hill mid-May to mid-Oct, Sat (call ahead). Shop

HIGHLIGHTS

● Bulfinch Federal design
● Reproductions of original wallpaper
● Yellow and turquoise paints
● Federal-era furniture

Museum of Science

- Lightning demo
- Virtual FishTank
- Natural Mysteries
- Mugar Omni Theater shows

TIPS

- Tickets for special exhibits often sell out during school vacation weeks. Buy in advance online.
- Arrive at least a half-hour early for Omni Theater shows to get the best seats.

This place buzzes and hums with excited children running around pressing buttons and peering into things. There are hundreds of interactive exhibits, as well as live presentations.

Science now The museum prides itself on being at the cutting edge of science education. The museum complex straddles the Charles River, with views of the Cambridge and Boston skylines.

"It's awesome" Don't miss the dramatic indoor lightning demos in the Theater of Electricity, where the world's largest Van de Graaff generator creates 2.5 million volts of electricity. Between shows, take part in the popular Virtual Volleyball exhibit. Close by, peer into the mouth of a T-Rex, modeled to reflect the latest paleontological theories.

Clockwise from far left: A father and son examine an exhibit at the museum; the blur of the fast-spinning wheels of a steam-powered engine; a crowded show in the Mugar Omni Theater; an interactive motion exhibit; the Butterfly Garden; the museum from the outside reflected in the Charles River

In the Virtual FishTank create a fish, then see how it interacts with other creatures when you release it into the ocean. Other popular exhibits include the Natural Mysteries, where you learn about scientific classification from collections of skulls, animal tracks, shells and more. Seeing is Deceiving explores both visual and auditory illusions, while in Science in the Park you can work out why a swing swings. There are also presentations at the Science Live! Stage.

Mugar Omni Theater and the Planetarium Lie back and be enveloped in the sight and sound of an IMAX movie in the five-story screen of the Mugar Omni Theater. Multimedia presentations at the Charles Hayden Planetarium cover astronomical subjects. Be dazzled by the evening laser shows that also take place here.

THE BASICS

www.mos.org

🕂 H3

✉ Science Park

☎ 617/723-2500

🕐 Jul 5–Labor Day Sat–Thu 9–7, Fri 9–9. Labor Day– Jul 4 Sat–Thu 9–5, Fri 9–9. Extended hours over school holidays

🍴 Three on premises

🚇 Science Park

♿ Excellent. Sight- and hearing-impaired facilities

💰 Expensive. Separate tickets for Planetarium, Laser Show, Omni Theater. Combination ticket discounts. Boston CityPass applies

❓ Good shop

HIGHLIGHTS

● Lion and unicorn
● Balcony from which the Declaration of Independence was read
● Exhibit showing topographical changes

TIPS

● Check the website for the latest events program.
● Don't miss the tiny phial of tea leaves saved from the Boston Tea Party.
● Light up the topographical map to see how much of Boston is built on landfill.

This is the city's oldest public building, once the seat of British colonial government. Surrounded by taller—but far less significant—buildings, it seems so tiny now. It holds a first-rate museum.

Colonial capital Built in 1713 to replace an earlier Town House, the Old State House was the British governor's seat of office, home to the judicial court and to the Massachusetts Assembly. As such it was the scene of many a confrontation between the colonists and their rulers. It was here that James Otis railed against the "tyranny of taxation without representation" and it was under the balcony at the east end that the "Boston Massacre" took place in 1770: Five colonists were killed in a clash with British soldiers, a key event in the years leading up to the Revolution. From the

The Puritan interior of the Old State House (below left) and the lion and unicorn on the east front (below)

same balcony, the Declaration of Independence was read on July 18, 1776, and is still read every July 4. At this point the gilded lion and unicorn on the east front, symbols of the British Crown, were destroyed. From 1780 until 1798, this was the Massachusetts State House. For most of the 19th century it was used for commercial purposes, gradually falling into disrepair until the Bostonian Society was founded in 1881 to restore it. The lion and the unicorn were returned to their place, balanced now by the American eagle and the Massachusetts seal.

A Museum of Boston The building is now home to the Bostonian Society's excellent museum, which traces the city's topographical, political, economic and social history, with a fine collection of maritime art and revolutionary memorabilia.

THE BASICS

www.bostonhistory.org

✚ K5

✉ 206 Washington Street

☎ 617/720-1713

🕐 Daily 9–5

🍴 Nearby

🚇 State, Government Center, Downtown Crossing

♿ No access to upper floor

👋 Inexpensive

❓ Shop

North End and Old North Church

HIGHLIGHTS

- Paul Revere House
  (▷ 34–35)
- Old North Church Steeple
- Copp's Hill Burying
  Ground (▷ 33)
- Feast-day processions
- Italian groceries, coffee
  shops and restaurants

TIP

- The North End explodes
  with life and color in late
  August for the Feast of
  St. Anthony.

The North End is Boston's oldest and most spirited district. This is where the British colonists settled in the 17th century, and now, after various ups and downs, it is a lively Italian quarter.

Little Italy The North End is separated from the rest of Boston by an area that was once a major highway, and is now a park. When the colonists arrived it was also all but cut off, surrounded then by water at the end of a narrow peninsula. The colonists' erratic street plan survives, but the only building from the 17th century is Paul Revere House. Once the elite had moved to Beacon Hill in the early 19th century, the area played host to waves of immigrants, first the Irish, then East Europeans and Portuguese, and finally Italians who have given the area its current flavor.

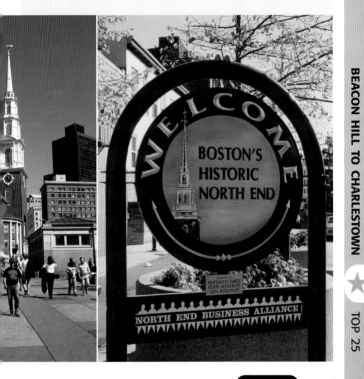

The equestrian statue of Paul Revere with St. Stephen's Church beyond (left); Old North Church is now overshadowed by office buildings (middle); the decorative sign that welcomes visitors to North End (below)

WELCOME

BOSTON'S HISTORIC NORTH END

NORTH END BUSINESS ALLIANCE

Paul Revere Mall On Hanover Street, opposite St. Stephen's Church, the mall connects the North End's main street to Old North Church. This tree-shaded park is James Rego Square, but locals call it the Prado. Standing at one end is a bronze equestrian statue of Paul Revere (▷ panel 125).

Old North Church It was from Old North that Revere's signal was given to the patriots in Charlestown that the British were on their way to Lexington where, the next day, the first battle of the War of Independence took place.

Copp's Hill Burying Ground Up the hill in front of Old North Church is a former Native American lookout point. In 1659 it became a burying ground, visited now for its rows of slate and stone headstones, many carved with winged skulls.

THE BASICS

✚ K4/K3
✉ Bounded by Commercial Street and Expressway
🕐 Old North Church: all year (steeple: Jun–Oct)
🍽 Plenty around Hanover and Salem streets
🚇 Haymarket, North Station, Aquarium, State
♿ Some hills and uneven sidewalks (pavements)

Paul Revere House

The bedroom (left) in Paul Revere House and views of the exterior (below right)

THE BASICS

www.paulreverehouse.org

K4

19 North Square

617/523-2338

Nov to mid-Apr daily 9.30–4.15; mid-Apr to Oct daily 9.30–5.15. Jan–Mar closed Mon

Nearby

Government Center, State, Aquarium, Haymarket

Wheelchair access first floor only

Inexpensive

Tours of early Georgian Pierce/Hichborn House

HIGHLIGHTS

● Revere's own account of his ride
● Period furnishings

TIPS

● Avoid the house on spring and fall (autumn) afternoons, when it is often overrun by school groups.
● Check ahead for the appearances by costumed interpreters.

This house is all that remains of the 17th-century settlement in today's North End. Not only is it Boston's oldest building, it was home to its most celebrated revolutionary, Paul Revere.

The early years The steep-gabled clapboard house that we see today was built in about 1680. Like most houses of the period, it had two rooms on each of its two floors but the positioning of the main staircase at the side of the building, making the rooms larger than normal, was unusual. By 1770, when the silversmith and engraver Paul Revere came to live here, significant alterations had been made, notably the addition of a third floor and a two-story extension at the back. The family lived here during the Revolution, so it was from here that Revere set out on that famous midnight ride (▷ panel 125). In 1800, after the family sold the house, it became a rooming house, with stores and factory premises on the lower floor. Threatened with demolition in 1902, it was saved by Revere's great-grandson, restored to something like its origins and became a museum.

The house today The basic timber skeleton of the house is the original, but the exterior clap-boarding, the windows and most of what you see inside are replacements. Go through the kitchen into the living room, furnished in period style. Upstairs, the main bedroom is an elegantly furnished room, which would have doubled as a parlor. In the other room, note the ingenious folding bed and its traditional woven cover.

State House (below) with its gleaming gold-leaf dome (right)

State House

Prosperous and newly independent in the late 18th century, Massachusetts needed a larger, more imposing State House. Charles Bulfinch's masterpiece is a landmark in American architecture.

Hub of the Hub Bulfinch began designing the new State House on his return from England, much influenced by Robert Adam's Renaissance style. Construction began in 1795 on a prominent piece of Beacon Hill land. Cut off in your mind's eye the side wings (an early 20th-century addition), and focus on Bulfinch's dignified two-story portico and the glistening dome. Its original shingles were covered in copper from the foundry of Paul Revere when the roof began to leak, and the gold leaf was added in 1874. Until skyscrapers arrived, it dominated the city skyline.

Seat of government Start your tour in the columned Doric Hall. From here pass through the marble Nurses' Hall and note Bela Pratt's memorial to Civil War nurses. The Italian marble floor in the Hall of Flags was laid by immigrants from Italy. Featured in the stained-glass skylight are the seals of the original 13 states. Up the staircase is the House of Representatives chamber. Here, the Sacred Cod, a symbol of the importance of the fishing industry and a lucky mascot, must hang whenever the 160 state representatives are in session. The dignified barrel-vaulted and Ionic-columned Senate Reception Room is Bulfinch's, as is the Senate Chamber, where 40 senators debate beneath a graceful sunburst dome.

THE BASICS

🔲 J5
✉ Beacon Street
☎ 617/727-3676
🕐 Mon–Fri 10–4 (except holiday Mondays)
🍴 None
Ⓟ Park Street
♿ Partial wheelchair access
🎟 Free
❓ Regular tours (45 min); last tour 3.30. It is advisable to call in advance to reserve a guided tour

HIGHLIGHTS

● Gold dome (regilded in 1997 with 22 carat gold leaf)
● Sacred Cod
● Senate Reception Room
● Senate Chamber
● JFK statue

TIP

● To enter the State House for tours use the side entrance on Bowdoin Street.

USS *Constitution* and Charlestown

HIGHLIGHTS

● Museum: details of a sailor's daily diet and duties
● USS *Constitution*: cramped lower deck

TIPS

● If you are walking the Freedom Trail from Boston, get here by 3pm to take a tour of the ship.
● Kids will love the top floor of the museum, where they can fire ships' cannons in interactive games.

"Old Ironsides," as she is widely known by schoolchildren, is the oldest commissioned warship afloat in the world. More than 200 years old, she is moored in the Charlestown Navy Yard.

The Navy Yard From 1800 to 1974 the Charlestown Navy Yard played an important role building, repairing and supplying Navy warships. Its mission now is to interpret the history of naval shipbuilding. Representing the ships built here are USS *Constitution* and the World War II destroyer USS *Cassin Young*, both of which may be boarded. The old granite Building 22 now houses the USS *Constitution* Museum, where journals and objects record the frigate's 200-year career in war and peace and give a picture of life aboard. Also open is the Commandant's House.

Gleaming cannons on the restored frigate USS Constitution, *"Old Ironsides" (left); the world's oldest commissioned battleship, at dock in Charlestown Navy Yard (middle top); details of the craftsmanship and rigging that have kept this venerable vessel afloat (middle below left and right, and below)*

THE BASICS

www.ussconstitution
museum.org

+ K2/J2

✉ Charlestown Navy Yard

☎ Navy Yard Visitor
Center: 617/242-5601.
"Whites of Their Eyes"
reservations: 617/241-7575

🕐 Museum: mid-Apr to
mid-Oct 9–6; mid-Oct to
mid-Apr 10–5
USS *Constitution*: Apr–Sep
Tue–Sun 10–4; Oct–Mar
Thu–Sat 10–3.30.
USS *Cassin Young*: daily
12–3 (Jul–Aug 10–5),
weather permitting; guided
tours daily 11, 2, 3.
Bunker Hill Monument:
daily 9–4.30 (Jul–Aug
9–5.30)
Base Lodge (toy soldier
battle display): daily 9–5.
Museum: May–Oct daily
9–6; Nov–Apr daily 10–5.
Bunker Hill Pavilion
"Whites of Their Eyes":
Apr–Nov daily 9.30–4

🍴 In the Navy Yard

Ⓟ North Station or
Community College, then
15-min walk

🚢 MBTA Water Shuttle
from Long Wharf

♿ All wheelchair
accessible except
USS *Cassin Young*

💵 All free except
"Whites of Their Eyes"
(inexpensive)

❓ Summer tours of Navy
Yard (11am)

The Bunker Hill Pavilion's multimedia show,
"Whites of Their Eyes," tells the story of the Battle
of Bunker Hill on which stands the Bunker Hill
Monument. This obelisk is visible from, and is
within walking distance of, the Navy Yard. Climb
its 294 steps for good views.

USS *Constitution* The highlight of the Yard is
"Old Ironsides." Launched in Boston in 1797,
she is still part of the US Navy, whose sailors lead
tours round the cramped quarters. Vulnerable
though the wooden sides seem now, it was her
tough live-oak frames that enabled her to survive
the War of 1812 undefeated and win her nick-
name. After surviving three wars, the vessel was
frail and needed to be heavily reconstructed.
She takes a turn in Boston Harbor every July 4,
changing the side that faces the elements.

More to See

AMES AND SEARS BUILDINGS

The 14-floor, 1889 Ames Building dominated the skyline until the Custom House Tower was built.

➕ K5 ✉ 1 Court Street 🚇 State

CHARLES RIVER BOAT TOURS

A leisurely cruise among the sailboats and crew teams on the Charles River offers a new perspective on the city, with views of Beacon Hill, the Boston skyline, the Esplanade and the Harvard residential houses. A 10am tour explores the locks and harbor.

➕ H3 ✉ 100 Cambridgeside Place, Suite 320, Cambridge ☎ 617/621-3001 🕐 10, 11.15, 12.30, 1.45, 3, 4.15, 5.30 and 7 🚇 Lechmere 💲 Expensive ❓ Main docking location at Canal Park, CambridgeSide Galleria, Cambridge

CHRISTOPHER COLUMBUS WATERFRONT PARK

This is a small waterfront park near Faneuil Hall Marketplace and North End. Buy a sandwich, sit under the trellis or on the grass and watch the boats.

➕ L4 ✉ Atlantic Avenue 🚇 Aquarium 🕐 Daily 💲 Free

CUSTOM HOUSE TOWER

The 30-floor clock tower (1915) is a Boston landmark and was for a long time the city's tallest building. At street level you see how silly it looks stuck on the roof of the original Custom House, built in 1847 in Greek Revival style, at what was then the water's edge. It is now a hotel, but the public can go up to the observatory for great views.

➕ K5 ✉ 3 McKinley Square 🕐 Observatory daily at 10 and 4, except Sat am 🚇 State, Aquarium 💲 Donation to charity

FLEETCENTER

www.fleetcenter.com

The old West End is not an exciting district, but has the FleetCenter, home to the Celtics and Bruins, next to North Station.

➕ J3 ✉ 150 Causeway Street ☎ Ticketmaster: 617/931-2000 🚇 North Station

The Custom House Tower at night

Commercial Wharf adjacent to Christopher Columbus Park on the waterfront

JAMES CURLEY STATUES

A colorful Boston Irish mayor, James Curley (1874–1958) comes both seated and standing (Lloyd Lillie, 1980).

✚ K4 ✉ North/Union streets 🚇 State

MUSEUM OF AFRO-AMERICAN HISTORY/BLACK HERITAGE TRAIL

www.afroammuseum.org

A museum dedicated to the history of African-Americans in Boston is housed in the African Meeting House, built in 1806 and the oldest surviving African-American church building in the US. Once a center for social and political activity, it is now a focal point on the Black Heritage Trail, a 1.6-mile (2.5km) guided or self-guided walking tour of pre-Civil War Beacon Hill sites, including the Abiel Smith School and the Robert Gould Shaw Monument.

✚ J5 ✉ 46 Joy Street ☎ 617/725-0022 ⏰ Memorial Day–Labor Day daily 10–4; rest of year: Mon–Fri 10–4 🚇 Charles/MGH, Park Street, Government Center 🎟 Free

NEW ENGLAND HOLOCAUST MEMORIAL

Six tall glass towers, the work of Stanley Saitowitz (1995), recall Nazi death camps. Etched numerals represent the Holocaust's 6 million victims. The memorial is especially poignant after dark, when it is floodlighted.

✚ K4 ✉ Union Street ⏰ Daily 🚇 State

NICHOLS HOUSE MUSEUM

www.nicholshousemuseum.org

One of Boston's earliest Federal-style houses, this elegant four-floor Beacon Hill house was built by Charles Bulfinch in 1804 and is furnished with Nichols family art and antiques.

✚ J5 ✉ 55 Mount Vernon Street ☎ 617/227-6993 ⏰ Apr–Oct Tue–Sat 12–4; Nov, Dec, Feb–Apr Thu–Sat 12–4. By tour only; last tour starts at 4pm 🚇 Park Street 🎟 Moderate

SAMUEL ADAMS STATUE

Anne Whitney's (1880) portrayal of the defiant revolutionary leader, in front of Faneuil Hall.

✚ K5 ✉ Congress Street 🚇 State

Statue of Paul Revere in front of the Old North Church (above)

The African Meeting House (right) hosts the Museum of Afro-American History

Freedom Trail

The Freedom Trail links the most significant sites from Boston's Colonial and revolutionary era. A red line on the sidewalk (pavement) makes it easy to follow.

DISTANCE: 1.5 miles (2.5km) **ALLOW:** 1–4 hours

START

BOSTON COMMON (▷ 50)
🚻 J5 🚇 Park Street

END

COPP'S HILL (▷ 32–33)
🚻 K3 🚇 North Station

❶ From the information center on Boston Common head for the State House (▷ 35). Walk down Park Street to "Brimstone Corner" where gunpowder was stored.

❽ Back in Hanover Street, turn onto Revere Mall, passing Paul Revere's statue (▷ 32–33), with the Old North Church (▷ 32) steeple ahead. Continue uphill to Copp's Hill.

❷ On Tremont Street, in the Old Granary Burying Ground, find the graves of many famous people. King's Chapel (▷ 55) is the oldest church site in Boston still in use.

❼ Cross Blackstone Street and cross the Rose Kennedy Greenway to the North End. Turn onto Richmond Street to reach North Square and Paul Revere House (▷ 34).

❸ On School Street a sidewalk mosaic marks the site of the first free school, open to all. Pass the statue of Benjamin Franklin.

❻ The trail continues between the New England Holocaust Memorial (▷ 39) and the Union Oyster House (▷ 46) to Hanover Street.

❹ Diagonally right, past the Irish Famine Memorial (▷ 55), is Old South Meeting House (▷ 56), where the Boston Tea Party started. Follow the red line along Washington Street to Old State House (▷ 30–31).

❺ Cross onto Congress Street to get to Faneuil Hall (▷ 26).

Shopping

BEACON HILL CHOCOLATES

Fine chocolate is transformed into delectable and beautiful gifts, packaged in elegant boxes. The tiny shop's entrance is just around the corner from Charles Street, perfectly located for a mid-shopping indulgence.
⊞ H5 ✉ 92B Pinckey Street ☎ 617/725-1900 Ⓜ Charles

BLACK INK

An eclectic selection of funky gifts and novelties: shark staplers, alphabet cookie cutters, bright green frog banks, architectural city guides.
⊞ H5 ✉ 101 Charles Street ☎ 617/723-3883
Ⓜ Charles/MGH, Arlington

BOSTON PEWTER COMPANY

All manner of traditional, hand-crafted pewter items fill shelves here, including pieces for the home (lighting, sculpture and dishes) and gift ware (picture frames, jewelry).
⊞ K5 ✉ South Market, Faneuil Hall Marketplace ☎ 617/523-1776 Ⓜ State, Government Center

BOSTONIAN HISTORICAL SOCIETY MUSEUM SHOP

Buy a little piece of New England history from this store created to support Boston's Historical Society. The group peddles books about New England's past, plus quilts, teas, mugs and prints.

⊞ K5 ✉ South Canopy, Faneuil Hall Marketplace ☎ 617/742-4744 Ⓜ State, Government Center

BUILD-A-BEAR WORKSHOP

Teddy bears are the focus, although this kid-pleasing shop has plush dinosaurs and other stuffed animals, too. Everything the well-dressed bear needs is here: clothes, holiday costumes, boots, paw brushes, Santa beards, furniture, sandals, ballet slippers and all the latest in bearwear.
⊞ K5 ✉ North Market, Faneuil Hall ☎ 617/227-2478 Ⓜ Government Center/State

CAMBRIDGESIDE GALLERIA

More than 120 stores and restaurants including Borders, Sears, Macy's, Best Buy, California Pizza Kitchen and the Cheesecake Factory.

THE CHAIN

Most of the major American clothes chains are represented in the city: Abercrombie & Fitch (Faneuil Hall Marketplace), Banana Republic (CambridgeSide Galleria, Newbury Street), French Connection, Gap, Giorgio Armani (Newbury Street), The Limited (Copley Place). British visitors will find familiar fashions at lower prices than back home.

⊞ G3 ✉ 100 CambridgeSide Place ☎ 617/621-8666 Ⓜ Lechmere

COACH

The sleek downtown outpost of the popular and high-quality international leather goods company sells an impressive selection of the collection's handbags, business gear, shoes and other accessories. Also at Copley Place.
⊞ K5 ✉ South Market, Faneuil Hall Marketplace ☎ 617/723-1777 Ⓜ State, Government Center

CRATE & BARREL

Well-designed, affordable household goods: Egyptian cotton sheets, table linen, hand-blown glass, kitchen utensils. Also at 777 Boylston Street, 48 Brattle Street and Copley Place.
⊞ K5 ✉ Faneuil Hall Marketplace ☎ 617/742-6025 Ⓜ State, Government Center

DANISH COUNTRY ANTIQUES

True to its name, this gem full of imported finds sells well-preserved, rustic pieces from Denmark. Don't miss the fine selection of tables—for the kitchen dining room, or living room.
⊞ H4 ✉ 138 Charles Street ☎ 617/227-4889 Ⓜ Charles

EUGENE GALLERIES

Specializes in old maps and prints, with a good selection covering Boston.

This is the place to discover heirlooms and excellent gifts.
➕ H5 ✉ 76 Charles Street
☎ 617/227-3062
🚇 Charles/MGH

FLAT OF THE HILL

One of the city's most charming gift boutiques, this is crammed with garden accessories, hand-knit throws, pretty stationery and more.
➕ H5 ✉ 60 Charles Street
☎ 617/619-9977 🚇 Charles

FOUR PREPPY PAWS

Everything imaginable and more, for that dog or cat (or maybe its owner).
➕ H5 ✉ 103 Charles Street
☎ 617/723-0112
🚇 Charles/MGH, Arlington

GEOCLASSICS

Geological wonders become fine jewelry, displayed to show their origin. For example, a necklace of quartz beads lies against a dramatic quartz crystal.
➕ K5 ✉ 7 North Market, Faneuil Hall ☎ 617/523-6112
🚇 Government Center/State

GOOD, INC

A range of simple but design-conscious gifts.
➕ H4 ✉ 88 Charles Street
☎ 617/722-9200 🚇 Charles

HILTON'S TENT CITY

Good place for hiking and a range of camping equipment and performance clothing.
➕ K4 ✉ 272 Friend Street

☎ 617/227-9242 🚇 North Station

HOLIDAY BOUTIQUE

Modern, sassy women's fashions line the racks of this small but well-stocked shop. Find moderately priced designs by Frost French, Lauren Moffatt, Petit Bateau, Cynthia Vincent and denim by Rock & Republic.
➕ H5 ✉ 53 Charles Street
☎ 617/973-9730 🚇 Charles

KOO DE KIR

The place to find housewares—from pitchers and calfskin rugs to transferware plates and star-shaped chandeliers—that are equal parts funky and classic. Home accessories and furniture from all over the globe.
➕ H5 ✉ 65 Chestnut Street
☎ 617/723-8111 🚇 Charles

LINENS ON THE HILL

Fine French linens—sheets, pillowcases, tablecloths. Also nightgowns and robes.
➕ H6 ✉ 52 Charles Street

CHARLES STREET

This is a delightful street of stores and restaurants, running north from the Public Garden through the flat area of Beacon Hill. It specializes in (mostly pricey) antiques shops but has several gift shops and galleries, too, and a selection of places where you can get a bite to eat.
➕ J4 🚇 Arlington, Charles

☎ 617/227-1255 🚇 Charles, Arlington

NOSTALGIA FACTORY

Film posters (some vintage), old signs, advertisements and more.
➕ K4 ✉ 51 North Margin Street (off Salem Street)
☎ 617/241-8300
🚇 Haymarket

RAND MCNALLY MAP & TRAVEL

Good range of maps and guides on New England and beyond. The stock holds atlases as well as globes and assorted geography-inspired gifts.
➕ K5 ✉ 84 State Street
☎ 617/720-1125 🚇 State

THE RED WAGON

Bright, creatively casual T-shirt sets, dresses and more for babies and young children.
➕ H5 ✉ 69 Charles Street
☎ 617/524-9402 🚇 Charles

SAVENOR'S

The late, mighty culinary queen Julia Child used to order her meats from this specialty foods market, where you'll find everything from giraffe meat to wild mushrooms.
➕ H5 ✉ 160 Charles Street
☎ 617/723-6328 🚇 Charles

WISH BOUTIQUE

A friendly, colorful women's clothing store, hung with frocks by Nanette Lapore, Rebecca Taylor and Theory.
➕ H5 ✉ 49 Charles Street
☎ 617/227-4441 🚇 Charles

Entertainment and Nightlife

21ST AMENDMENT

www.21stboston.com
Across from the State House, a good spot to refuel with beer and pressed sandwiches while walking the Freedom Trail. At night, it attracts a young local crowd.

J5 ⊠ 150 Bowdoin Street
☎ 617/227-7100
Bowdoin, Park Street

THE BLACK ROSE

www.irishconnection.com/blackrose
This family Irish bar is one of the best places to catch live Celtic music—and line your stomach with corned beef and Guinness.

J5 ⊠ 160 State Street
☎ 617/742-2286 State

CHEERS

www.cheersboston.com
After standing in line for hours, tourists are often disappointed that the inside of the Bull & Finch on Beacon Hill, which served as the model for the television show *Cheers*, looks nothing like it does on TV. Instead, go by the new Cheers bar in Faneuil Hall, which was designed to an exact replica of the set.

K5 ⊠ 84 Beacon Street / Faneuil Hall Marketplace
☎ 617/227-9605 or 617/227-0150
Charles/MGH, Arlington, Haymarket

COMEDY CONNECTION

www.comedyconnection/boston.com
A first-class comedy club, with shows every night. Reserve ahead.

K5 ⊠ Faneuil Hall Marketplace ☎ 617/248- 9700
Shows Mon–Wed 8pm; Thu 8.30pm; Fri–Sat 8, 10.15pm; Sun 7pm
State, Government Center

HONG KONG AT FANEUIL HALL

www.hongkongboston.com
Two words: scorpion bowls! The booze-filled punch packs a wallop, and fuels a fun but cheesy dance scene.

K5 ⊠ 65 Chatham Street
☎ 617/227-2226 State

NIGHTLIFE AND CRUISES

Odyssey
Operates evening cruises on a 600-passenger yacht, plus a Sunday jazz brunch and weekday lunches (reservations required).

⊠ Rowes Wharf
☎ 617/654-9710 or 888/741-0281;
www.odyssey.com

The Spirit of Boston
Has live bands and shows on its dinner-dance cruises.

⊠ World Trade Center
☎ 617/748-1450;
www.spiritcruises.com
Lunch and dinner cruises daily Jun–Oct

IMPROV ASYLUM

www.improvasylum.com
Two venues for improvisational comedy at a North End cabaret-style theater and in a larger Theater District club.

K4 ⊠ 216 Hanover Street
☎ 617/263-6887
Shows Wed–Sat
Haymarket

LAST HURRAH

www.omnihotels.com
Black-and-white photos from Boston's Golden Age line the walls in the Parker House's upscale hotel bar. Clientele is a mix of hotel guests and City Hall politicos.

K5 ⊠ 60 School Street
☎ 617/227-8600
Government Center, State

SILVERTONE BAR & GRILL

A stylish subterranean bar that draws a mixed crowd of students and professionals for specialty cocktails and gooey comfort food. Crowded on weekends.

K5 ⊠ 68 Bromfield Street
☎ 617/338-7887
Park Street

SEVENS

Often referred to as the "real Cheers," this Charles Street institution draws a slice from all walks of life to drink frosty ones at wooden booths and gripe about the Sox.

H5 ⊠ 77 Charles Street
☎ 617/523-9074
Charles/MGH

INSPIRATION
FOR THE
TV SERIES

Cheers

BULL & FINCH

PUB

CELEBRATING OUR
30th ANNIVERSARY

BULL & FINCH
PUB

HAMPSHIRE HOUSE

Restaurants

PRICES

Prices are approximate, based on a 3-course meal for one person.
$$$ over $40
$$ $20–$40
$ under $20

ANTICO FORNO ($)

Excellent Italian specialties abound at this casual, small spot, all whisked from the brick oven to your table. Don't miss fusilli with vegetables, goat cheese and basil, or the swordfish with citrus and pickled onions.
K4 ⊠ 296 Hanover Street ☎ 617/227-7606 🕐 Lunch Mon–Sat; dinner daily 🚇 Haymarket

ARTÙ ($)

Country-style Italian cooking and friendly staff. Try chicken layered with eggplant and mozzarella. There is a second branch at 89 Charles Street.
K4 ⊠ 6 Prince Street, North End ☎ 617/742-4336 🕐 From 11am 🚇 Haymarket

BEACON HILL BISTRO ($$)

A soothing, neutral-toned bistro serving excellent seafood dishes and a creative late-night bar menu. Don't miss top-notch desserts like the rhubarb clafouti with macerated strawberries and milk-flavored ice cream.
H5 ⊠ 25 Charles Street ☎ 617/723-7575 🚇 Charles/MGH

CAFFÈ VITTORIA ($)

Popular North End spot for an after-dinner coffee, pastry or *gelato*.
K4 ⊠ 296 Hanover Street ☎ 617/227-7606 🚇 Haymarket

CANTINA ITALIANA ($$)

A relaxed eatery serving excellent regional food.
K4 ⊠ 346 Hanover Street, North End ☎ 617/723-4577 🕐 Mon–Sat from 4; Sun from noon 🚇 Haymarket

DURGIN PARK ($$)

www.durgin-park.com
One of the oldest dining rooms in the US. The roast beef melts in the mouth and there's hard-to-find traditional fare like Indian pudding. Crowded; very informal—but the waiters make a thing of being rude.
K5 ⊠ Faneuil Hall Marketplace ☎ 617/227-2038 🕐 Mon–Sat 11–10, Sun

SEAFOOD OPTIONS

Nowadays some of Boston's finest fish is served outside of the traditional seafood restaurants listed on these pages. Most of the city's best eating spots do an excellent job with seafood preparations, and these dishes are taking an increasingly large share of their menus. Other good choices for fresh seafood are any of the Chinatown restaurants with live-from-the-tanks fish.

11.30–9 🚇 State, Aquarium, Government Center

HUNGRY I ($$$)

Tiny, intimate basement offering a small but inventive menu.
H5 ⊠ 71 Charles Street, Beacon Hill ☎ 617/227-3524 🕐 Lunch Thu–Fri; dinner Tue–Sun; brunch Sun 🚇 Charles/MGH

KINGFISH HALL ($$–$$$)

www.toddenglish.com
Flashy Faneuil Hall fish joint. Creative, if pricey, fish dishes in an eclectic modern (often noisy) room.
K5 ⊠ 188 S. Market Street ☎ 617/523-8862 🕐 Lunch Mon–Sat; dinner daily; brunch Sun 🚇 State, Government Center

LA FAMIGLIA GIORGIO'S RESTAURANT ($$)

All the favorites, in generous portions, are served at this family-friendly Roman-style restaurant. Teachers and students with ID get 20 percent discount, and the children's menu offers more choices than most.
K4 ⊠ 112 Salem Street ☎ 617/367-6711 🕐 Lunch and dinner daily 🚇 Haymarket

LALA ROKH ($$)

Refined Persian cuisine fills the menu at this casually elegant, low-ceilinged restaurant. Specialties include exotic

45

creations like chicken with rose petals, cumin and cinnamon. The saffron ice cream is a must-try.
➕ H5 ✉ 97 Mount Vernon Street ☎ 617-720-5511 🚇 Charles/MGH

MAMMA MARIA ($$$)
www.mammamaria.com
Highly regarded elegant North End Italian, offering imaginative cooking and gracious service. Try the *osso buco* (traditional shin of veal stew).
➕ K4 ✉ 3 North Square, North End ☎ 617-523-0077 🕐 Dinner daily 🚇 Haymarket

NAPOLI PASTRY SHOP ($)
In summer the floor-to-ceiling widows of this shop open to make it a sidewalk café. The cakes and cannoli are made on the premises, perfect accompaniments for a steaming cappuccino; the *gelato* is excellent.
➕ K4 ✉ 120 Salem Street ☎ 617-742-0809 🕐 Daily 7am–11pm 🚇 Haymarket

NO. 9 PARK ($$$)
New American fare in a dignified if simple dining room. Chef Barbara Lynch has a way with duck; her signature crispy duck is deliciously crisp outside, meltingly tender within. Less expensive café menu.
➕ J5 ✉ 9 Park Street ☎ 617/742-9991 🕐 Lunch Mon–Fri; dinner Mon–Sat 🚇 Park Street

PLAZA III, THE KANSAS CITY STEAKHOUSE ($$)
www.plazathreeboston.com
A white-lineened dining room sets the scene for civilized steakhouse dining. Lunches get particularly busy, as the neighboring Financial District employees file in. ➕ K5 ✉ 101 South Market Building, Faneuil Hall Marketplace ☎ 617-720-5570 🕐 Lunch Mon–Sat; dinner daily 🚇 State, Government Center

PREZZA ($$$)
www.prezza.com
Modern Italian fare in a hip space. Try the homemade pastas such as pea tortelli with Virginia ham. Save room for the chocolate hazelnut cake.
➕ L4 ✉ 24 Fleet Street, North End ☎ 617-227-1577 🕐 Dinner Mon–Sat 🚇 Haymarket

SLUGGER'S DUGOUT ($)
www.sluggersdugout.com
If you're dying for a good ol' burger (black angus

NEW ENGLAND DISHES
Try these: lobster, clam chowder, scrod, quahog (a large clam, pronounced "ko hog"), Boston baked beans (cooked long and slow in an earthenware pot), Boston cream pie (chocolate-covered and custard-filled white cake), Indian pudding (cornmeal, milk and molasses, cooked long and slow).

beef) or bit of ice cream (flavors such as black raspberry and bubble gum), head to Slugger's.
➕ K5 ✉ Quincy Market Building, Faneuil Hall Marketplace ☎ 617-723-3635 🕐 Lunch daily; dinner daily 🚇 State, Government Center

SULTAN'S KITCHEN ($)
Turkish-Middle Eastern takeout (with a few tables), convenient for lunch or early dinner; good vegetarian dishes, salads and kebabs.
➕ K5 ✉ 72 Broad Street, Financial District ☎ 617-338-7819 🕐 Mon–Fri 11–8; Sat 11–3 🚇 Aquarium

UNION OYSTER HOUSE ($$)
More regarded as an historic landmark than as eatery, Union Oyster House has been open since 1826, and has hosted everyone from John F. Kennedy to Leonardo DiCaprio.
➕ K4 ✉ 41 Union Street ☎ 617-227-2750 🚇 Haymarket

UPPER CRUST PIZZERIA ($)
Uncommonly good, gourmet pizzas are created here—all thin-crusted, and all straight out of the oven. The Margherita is a favorite, but don't bypass other toppings such as baby clams, prosciutto, asiago and pineapple.
➕ H5 ✉ 20 Charles Street, ☎ 617-723-9600 🚇 Charles

The bustling area running from Boston Common and the Public Garden to the Waterfront takes you through the Theater District, Chinatown and the Financial District.

Boston Common to the Waterfront

Aquarium

**New England
Aquarium**

INDIA STREET

ROSE

KENNEDY

Broad Street

battery March St

Milk Street

Milk
St

Hawes Street

Franklin Street

Wendell Street

**Post
Office
Square**

**Art Deco
Skyscrapers**

High

Oliver St

**Verizon
Building**
DISTRICT

GREENWAY

AVENUE

NORTHERN AVE

BRIDGE

EVELYN MOAKLEY

BRIDGE

Street

NORTHERN

**Federal Reserve
Bank of Boston**

ATLANTIC

Aid

St

Estes Pl

Gilbert Pl

CONGRESS STREET

BRIDGE

**Children's
Museum**

NEW

Sleeper Street

Fairnsworth Street

NORTHERN

AVENUE

Boston Inner Harbor

**Harbor Lights
Pavilion**

**Institute of
Contemporary Art**

AVENUE

AVENUE

South
Station

**BOSTON
SOUTH
STATION**

**Boston Tea Party
Ship & Museum**

SUMMER ST

BRIDGE

DORCHESTER AVENUE

Melcher St

Fort Point

Pittsburgh St

**Boston Fire
Museum**

Stillings Street

CONGRESS

STREET

0   250 m

0   250 yds

L   M

Boston Common and Public Garden

TOP 25

Pedal-powered Swan Boats, which date from 1877, transport visitors across the pond in the Public Garden

Very different in history and character, these adjoining pieces of public open space, separated by Charles Street, right in the heart of the city, are held in deep affection. Without them, Boston just wouldn't be Boston.

Boston Common The oldest public park in the US owes its origins to early British settlers who in 1634 acquired the land from a Reverend William Blaxton for common grazing. It was also where criminals were hanged, witches were dunked, and the dead were buried (in the Central Burying Ground, by Boylston Street). Here, British soldiers camped and George Washington addressed the crowds after Independence. Early in the 1800s paths were laid out, and fountains and monuments erected. It is still a place for speeches and demonstrations, but also for street performers and concerts or, in winter, ice-skating at Frog Pond. Safe by day, it's best avoided at night.

The Public Garden Much more genteel and decorative, this was created as a botanical garden in 1837. Hundreds of trees were planted, and beds, lawns and a lacing of footpaths were laid out. The garden is perennially beautiful and often fairy-tale-like. The focal point is a pond, with a pretty little cast-iron suspension bridge (the world's smallest). Here, in summer, you can ride the famous Swan Boats. Sculptures include a striking equestrian George Washington (Thomas Ball, 1869) and the Ether Monument, marking the first use of ether as an anaesthetic, here in Boston, in 1846.

Boston Athenaeum

Many Bostonians have never been here. You must see what they are missing. Leave 21st-century hassle behind and enter what Henry James called "the haunt of all the most civilized."

Temple of culture When the Athenaeum library moved to 101/2 Beacon Street in 1849 it had been the center of intellectual and cultural life in Boston for more than 40 years. Indeed, the paintings and sculptures it had accumulated formed the core of the Museum of Fine Arts' original collection. Founded in 1807 to foster scholarship, literature, science and the visual arts, it remains the haunt of Boston's intellectual elite. Extensions and refurbishment have restored the building to its former glory and brought its facilities into the 21st century. The collection of 600,000 volumes includes George Washington's personal library.

Silence Visitors have access to the first floor at any time and to other floors by guided tour. Many of the library's important paintings hang in a large first-floor gallery. Glass walls screen a newspaper and magazine reading room. A splendid old elevator (complemented by a modern one) takes members up to the second-floor reading room and print room, a third-floor room where members browse and converse, and a silent fifth-floor research room. On all floors long windows overlook the Old Granary Burying Ground, leather-upholstered chairs are drawn up to antique tables, oriental rugs cover the floors, books line the walls, busts and statues stand on plinths.

THE BASICS

www.bostonathenaeum.org

🔢 J5

✉ 101/2 Beacon Street

☎ 617/227-0270

🕐 First floor: Mon 8.30–8, Tue–Fri 9–5.30; also Sep–May Sat 9–4.
Other floors: by tour only, Tue, Thu 3pm (you must reserve ahead)

🍴 Nearby

🚇 Park Street

♿ Wheelchair access

💷 Free

❓ Lectures, concerts

HIGHLIGHTS

● The civilized, unhurried atmosphere
● The reading rooms
● Paintings and sculptures
● Views of Old Granary Burying Ground

TIP

● Stop by the Athenaeum on Tuesday or Thursday at 3pm for a docent tour of all five floors of the library. Call ahead to reserve a space.

Institute of Contemporary Art

TOP 25

The superb new home of the Institute (left); The Founders' Gallery (below)

Until the opening of this stunning building in December 2006, there was little reason for visitors to cross the Fort Point Channel into South Boston's waterfront district. Now there are several: the structure itself, the collection and HarborWalk.

The building The first US work of the architectural firm of Diller Scofidio + Renfro, the dramatic building reaches out over the harbor with a breathtaking cantilevered facade. Its expanses of glass overlook superb views, and the area sheltered by the overhang creates an amphitheater for performances with the water as a backdrop.

The art Superb though the views may be, the building also offers extraordinary opportunities for displaying contemporary art and mounting multimedia presentations. The Institute's permanent collection of 21st-century art includes works by leading names, among them Philip-Lorca diCorcia, Mona Hatoum, Ambreen Butt, Paul Chan, Rineke Dijkstra and Thomas Hirschorn. As the museum's holdings continue to grow, the main emphasis is on the well-interpreted special exhibitions that explore the complex nature of artistic expression.

HarborWalk Part of a planned 47-mile (76km) promenade that will cover Boston's entire waterfront, the section of HarborWalk that connects Rowe's Wharf to the Institute, is worth walking for its own art. In addition to the harbor views, the walkway is lined with beautiful iron sculptures representing marine themes.

The modern concrete structure of the aquarium (right) and a replica coral reef home to tropical fish (below)

New England Aquarium

One of the largest aquatic collections in the world, this is a popular family excursion. A spiral ramp leads you around a vast cylindrical tank swirling with sea creatures of every imaginable size, shape and hue.

Penguins, sharks and electric eels In the penguin pool at the base of the Giant Ocean Tank pick out the world's smallest species, the Little Blues, then head left, past the Medical Center. Either go outside for a sea-lion presentation or turn right, up the straight ramp, to the Thinking Gallery, where you can compare your hearing to that of a dolphin and your skeleton to that of a fish. The Freshwater Gallery has above- and below-surface views of a flooded Amazon forest complete with anaconda, alongside, by contrast, a New England trout stream. Don't miss the electric eel. Eventually, you reach the top of the huge tank at the heart of the Aquarium. At feeding times, approximately hourly, staff dive in, scattering squid for the bigger fish, jamming lettuce into the fiberglass coral reef for the angel fish, hand-feeding the sharks and giving the turtles their vitamin-enriched gelatin (to keep their shells hard). Notice how all the fish swim in the same direction, into the current set up by the filter, to get more oxygen.

From big screen to deep waters To experience places that cannot be re-created in the aquarium, watch one of the aquatic films showing at the IMAX theater. Alternatively, take the excellent Voyager III whale-watching trip.

THE BASICS

www.neaq.org

⊕ L5

✉ Central Wharf

☎ 617/973-5200

🕐 Jul 1–Labor Day Mon–Thu 9–6, Fri–Sun, holidays 9–7; rest of year Mon–Fri 9–5, Sat, Sun, holidays 9–6

🍽 On premises

♿ Aquarium 🕭 Good

💲 Expensive (IMAX is extra). Boston CityPass applies

❓ Concerts, lectures, tours, shop, whale-watching Apr–Oct ☎ 617/973-5281

HIGHLIGHTS

● Giant Ocean Tank
● Medical Center
● The huge green sea turtle
● Little Blue penguins
● Whale-watching trip
● IMAX 3D films

TIPS

● Book two weeks in advance for a special "behind the scenes" family tour ($12 per person).
● On Saturday, kids can solve mysteries of the deep in "Ocean Detective" classes.

More to See

ADAMS GALLERY

The history and culture of Boston and New England provides plenty of themes for collections and exhibits in this storefront gallery opposite Park Street Church (▷ 56). Everything from the Red Sox to home milk delivery have been featured in this interesting stop along the Freedom Trail.

➕ J5 ✉ Suffolk University Law School, 120 Tremont Street ☎ 617/305-1782 🕐 Daily 9–7 🚇 Park Street

ARLINGTON STREET CHURCH

If the church is closed, ask the staff in the office (at the back) if it can be opened up. It has the largest collection of Tiffany windows in any one church.

➕ H6 ✉ Boylston Street at Arlington Street. Office: 351 Boylston Street 🕐 Office: Mon–Thu 9–4 🚇 Arlington

ART DECO SKYSCRAPERS

There are four landmark art deco buildings in and around Post Office Square. On the corner of Water and Congress, note the elaborate facade of the John W. McCormack Post Office and Court House (1931). In Federal Street (at Franklin), the old State Street Bank, 70–75, has an external metalwork frieze and splendid metalwork in the lobby at 75–101. At 160 Federal, the United Shoe Machinery Building (1929) has exciting metalwork in and out. Also, look for No. 60 Battery March Street, now Hilton Financial District (1928).

➕ K5 🚇 State, Downtown Crossing, Aquarium

CHILDREN'S MUSEUM

This museum is heaven on earth for the under-10s. Try the balance climb, play at shops with life-size products, squirt water jets at model boats, stretch a gigantic bubble or just enjoy the play space. And when you're all exhausted, retreat to the peace and quiet of the Japanese house.

➕ L6 ✉ 300 Congress Street, Museum Wharf ☎ 617/426-8855 🕐 Daily 10–5 (Fri until 9) 🍽 Several nearby 🚇 South Station 💵 Moderate (Fri 5–9 $1)

Colorful neon lights inside the Children's Museum

CHINATOWN

Although small, the blocks between the Financial District and Kneeland Street is so intensely Asian that it's hard to believe it's still downtown Boston. The third largest Chinese community in the United States keeps the grocery stores, markets and bakeries thriving, and visitors join them to keep its many restaurants humming.

🛟 J6 🚇 Chinatown, South Station

FEDERAL RESERVE BANK OF BOSTON

www.bos.frb.org
The bank hosts free concerts most Thursdays, September to December and March to June.

🛟 L6 ✉ 600 Atlantic Avenue, opposite South Station ☎ 617/913-3453 ⓒ Concerts at 12.30 🚇 South Station

IRISH FAMINE MEMORIAL

These 1998 bronzes commemorate those forced by the 1840s Potato Famine to leave their native Ireland.

🛟 K5 ✉ Washington/School streets

KING'S CHAPEL AND BURYING GROUND

This was built as an Anglican church in 1687 on the orders of King James II, to the indignation of the Puritan colonists. In the town's earliest (1630) burial ground lie two *Mayflower* passengers and John Winthrop, first governor of Massachusetts.

🛟 K5 ✉ Tremont/School streets ⓒ Daily. No tourists during services 🚇 Park Street

OLD GRANARY BURYING GROUND

If you see only one burial ground, make it this one. Dating from 1660, it's the leafy resting place of many of Boston's big names—Samuel Adams, Paul Revere, James Otis, John Hancock, Peter Faneuil. Throughout, informative sign boards add historic information about the carved head-stones, the people buried here and events that shaped early Boston. Many of these add little-known sidelights to the 'school book' history, bringing the place and the Colonial era to life.

🛟 J5 ✉ 88 Tremont Street 🚇 Park Street

King's Chapel later became the city's first Unitarian Church

OLD SOUTH MEETING HOUSE

Starting life in 1729 as a Puritan meeting house, it was the site of the meeting that started the Boston Tea Party in 1773. Visual and audio exhibits.

➕ K5 ✉ 310 Washington Street ☎ 617/482 -6439 🕐 Apr–Oct daily 9.30–5; Nov–Mar daily 10–5 🚇 State, Downtown Crossing ✋ Moderate

PARK STREET CHURCH

Notable as much for its tall white steeple as for William Lloyd Garrison's first anti-slavery speech made here in 1829. "America the Beautiful" was first sung in public here in 1831. An excellent stop for architecture lovers.

➕ J5 ✉ 1 Park Street 🕐 Jul–Aug Tue–Sat 8.30–3.30 🚇 Park Street ✋ Free

POST OFFICE SQUARE

A charming oasis, with a small café, surrounded by the Downtown area's skyscrapers. It's often filled with office workers come lunchtime, however; arrive in late morning or late afternoon to get a park bench and best appreciate the sights and sounds.

➕ K5 ✉ Between Milk and Franklin streets 🚇 State

ROBERT GOULD SHAW MEMORIAL

A sensitive bronze battle frieze by Augustus Saint-Gaudens built in 1897 in honor of the Massachusetts 54th Regiment. Shaw, depicted in the film *Glory*, led the Union's first black regiment in the Civil War. Here, for the first time, blacks were portrayed by a white artist as individuals.

➕ J5 ✉ Beacon Street, facing State House 🚇 Park Street ✋ Free

VERIZON BUILDING

This 1940s art deco structure (formerly the Bell Atlantic/New England Telephone building) dominates Post Office Square. In the lobby, a 1950s mural (by Dean Cornwell) and a re-creation of Alexander Graham Bell's workshop celebrate the invention (in Boston) of the telephone.

➕ K5 ✉ 185 Franklin ☎ 617/743-4747 🕐 Mon–Fri 8–6 🚇 State, Downtown Crossing ✋ Free

Old South Meeting House

Pausing for a rest at the base of the Robert Gould Shaw Monument

Walk This Way

The areas around Boston Common and the Waterfront are some of the most pedestrian-friendly, with historic stops and shopping.

DISTANCE: 0.8 miles (1.2km) **ALLOW:** 2–4 hours

START

END

BOSTON COMMON
(▷ 50) ✚ J6 🚇 Boylston

NEW ENGLAND AQUARIUM
(▷ 53) ✚ L5 🚇 Aquarium

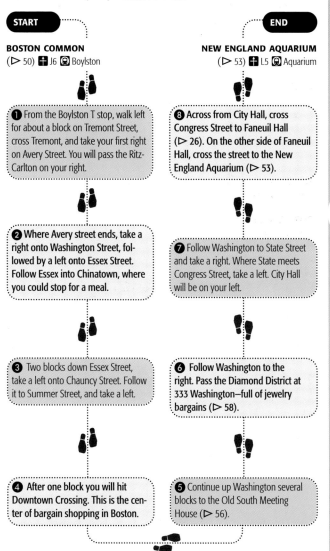

1 From the Boylston T stop, walk left for about a block on Tremont Street, cross Tremont, and take your first right on Avery Street. You will pass the Ritz-Carlton on your right.

8 Across from City Hall, cross Congress Street to Faneuil Hall (▷ 26). On the other side of Faneuil Hall, cross the street to the New England Aquarium (▷ 53).

2 Where Avery street ends, take a right onto Washington Street, followed by a left onto Essex Street. Follow Essex into Chinatown, where you could stop for a meal.

7 Follow Washington to State Street and take a right. Where State meets Congress Street, take a left. City Hall will be on your left.

3 Two blocks down Essex Street, take a left onto Chauncy Street. Follow it to Summer Street, and take a left.

6 Follow Washington to the right. Pass the Diamond District at 333 Washington—full of jewelry bargains (▷ 58).

4 After one block you will hit Downtown Crossing. This is the center of bargain shopping in Boston.

5 Continue up Washington several blocks to the Old South Meeting House (▷ 56).

Shopping

BRATTLE BOOKSHOP

A treasure trove of rare and secondhand books with a good section on Boston and New England. This family-owned and -run shop has been in business since the 19th century. So count on finding plenty of out-of-print and rare books, plus academic works, maps and old leather-bound books.

🔟 J5 ✉ 9 West Street
☎ 617/542-0210
🅿 Park Street

BROMFIELD PEN SHOP

Pens, from vintage early 1900s models to new Montblanc, Cross and cheap disposables.

🔟 J5 ✉ 5 Bromfield Street
☎ 617/482-9053
🅿 Park Street

DOWNTOWN CROSSING

Stores selling street fashion, shoes, jewelry, cameras and the like, plus the city's main department stores. Encompassing part of Washington, Winter and Bromfield streets, Downtown Crossing is mainly pedestrians-only.

🔟 J6 🅿 Downtown Crossing

FOOT PATHS

Elegant shoes for men and women, plus a full range of hiking boots. Also at 131 State Street.

🔟 K6 ✉ 489 Washington Street ☎ 617/338-6008
🅿 Downtown Crossing

THE ICA STORE

Arguably the most exciting design gift shop in Boston, the ICA Store carries a stunning selection of jewelry, household decor items, children's toys, accessories and books on contemporary art and design.

🔟 L6 ☎ 617/478-3104 ✉ 100 Northern Avenue 🕐 Tue–Wed, Sat–Sun 10–5, Thu–Fri 10–9 🅿 Courthouse

LOUIS BOSTON

High-quality, expensive and cutting-edge clothing for men and women in a spacious old mansion just off Newbury Street. Additionally, find international housewares, a small bookstore, plenty of accessories, a bridal registry, a hair salon and a DJ spinning station. There is also a lovely restaurant on the premise—all of which adds up to one of Boston's most fashionable addresses.

DOWNTOWN BARGAINS

Downtown Crossing, and all around Washington Street, is known as prime bargain territory for the marked-down jewelry sold at the **Diamond District** (at 333 Washington Street). Other discounts nearby: designer men's and women's shoes at DSW Shoe (385 Washington Street) outdoor gear at Eddie Bauer Outlet (500 Washington Street).

🔟 H6 ✉ 234 Berkeley Street
☎ 617/262-6100
🅿 Arlington

ST. JOHN BOUTIQUE

St. John was founded 43 years ago by Robert and Marie Gray and now has stores all over the globe. Elegant, couture knitwear for women.

🔟 H6 ✉ 292 Boylston Street
☎ 617/338-6130
🅿 Arlington

SKECHERS

Very cool men's, women's and kids' athletic shoes, boots, sneakers and sandals.

🔟 J5 ✉ 417 Washington Street ☎ 617/423-0412
🅿 Downtown Crossing

TANNERY

With a staff dedicated to finding the perfect fit for each and every customer's foot, this is the place to pick up both rugged outdoor shoes and casual numbers alike. Wide range of hiking boots and sneakers (Vans, Timberland, Sebago, Rockport). Also in Brattle Street, Harvard Square.

🔟 H6 ✉ 400 Boylston Street
☎ 617/267-0899
🅿 Arlington

Entertainment and Nightlife

AQUA
www.aquaboston.com
A watering hole for young professionals draws a hip crowd for mood lighting, martinis and DJs on weekends.
➕ K5 ✉ 120 Water Street
☎ 617/720-4900 🚇 State

BOSTON OPERA HOUSE
www.bostonoperahouse.com
Originally a vaudeville theater, this grand showroom was beautifully restored in 2004. It now features the biggest Broadway touring productions, as well as the Boston Ballet's annual performances of the *Nutcracker*.
➕ K6 ✉ 539 Washington Street ☎ 617/931-2787
🚇 Chinatown, Boylston

CHARLES PLAYHOUSE
Shear Madness, a comedy whodunnit set in a hairdresser's, has played here since 1980. *Blue Man Group*, another long-running show, presents its offbeat mix of theater, music and performance art on the Charles' other stage.
➕ J6 ✉ 74 Warrenton Street
☎ 617/426-5225 *(Shear Madness)*; 617/426-6912 (*Blue Man Group*) 🚇 Boylston

CLUB EUROPA
On the line between the South End and the Theater District, this toplevel nightclub is open from Thursday through Saturday. Thursday is Latin night, dance hall night is on Friday and Saturday is gay men's night.
➕ H6 ✉ 51 Stuart Street
☎ 617/482-3939 ⏰ Thu–Sat
🚇 Boylston

COLONIAL THEATRE
This lush, beautifully restored, turn-of-the-19th-century theater stages pre-Broadway productions as well as a range of other performing arts events.
➕ J6 ✉ 106 Boylston Street
☎ 617/426-9366
🚇 Boylston

CUTLER MAJESTIC THEATRE
www.maj.org
Visiting dance troupes, world music performers, Shakespearean actors and Emerson College student productions all use the stage at this 1903 venue.
➕ J6 ✉ 219 Tremont Street
☎ 617/824-8000
🚇 Boylston

DICK DOHERTY'S COMEDY VAULT
www.dickdoherty.com
A leading comedy club, in a former bank vault.
➕ J6 ✉ 124 Boylston Street
☎ 800/401-2221
⏰ Shows Thu–Sun
🚇 Boylston

EMMANUEL CHURCH
www.emmanuelmusic.org
A Bach cantata every Sunday (September through May).
➕ H6 ✉ 15 Newbury Street
☎ 617/536-3356
🚇 Arlington

FELT
www.feltboston.com
A pool hall cum dance club in the heart of Downtown, this multilevel nightspot features swanky decor, well-dressed patrons and regular appearances by local VIPs.
➕ K6 ✉ 533 Washington Street ☎ 617/350-5555
🚇 Downtown Crossing

THE GOOD LIFE
www.goodlifebar.com
A stylish lounge offers a menu of gourmet pizzas and small plates for sharing. More than 125 varieties of vodka at the frozen vodka bar.
➕ K6 ✉ 28 Kingston Street
☎ 617/451-2622
🚇 Chinatown

TICKETS
BosTix sell half-price theater tickets on the day of the show (from 11am). As a fully fledged Ticketmaster outlet, it also sells full-price tickets in advance for venues in Boston and the rest of New England. Booths are at: ✉ Faneuil Hall Marketplace 🕐 Tue–Sat 10–6, Sun 11–4; ✉ Copley Square 🕐 Mon–Sat 10–6, Sun 11–4.
Tickets cover theater, concerts, museums, sports events and trolley tours. All are sold for cash only.

GYPSY BAR
www.gypsybarboston.com
Sultry interior, an intimate dance floor and events such as lingerie fashion shows combine for the city's sexiest pick-up scene.
✚ J6 ✉ 116 Boylston
☎ 617/482-7799
🚇 Boylston

INSTITUTE OF CONTEMPORARY ART (ICA)
www.icaboston.org
An exhibition, film and performance space (▷ 52).
✚ M6 ✉ 100 Northern Avenue 🚇 Courthouse

JACQUE'S CABARET
And now for something completely different… Female impersonators and other offbeat performances draw everyone from drag queens to bachelorette parties.
✚ J6 ✉ 79 Broadway
☎ 617/426-8902
🚇 Arlington

JER-NE BAR
Picture windows line the walls of Ritz-Carlton's lavish hotel bar, the better for passersby to see you sipping a high-priced martini with the beautiful people.
✚ J6 ✉ 10 Avery Street
☎ 617/574-7100 🚇 Boylston

J. J. FOLEY'S
One of the last working-man's Irish bars downtown—it ain't pretty, but it's authentic. And the drinks come cheap.
✚ K6 ✉ 21 Kingston Street
☎ 617/338-7713
🚇 Downtown Crossing

NICK'S COMEDY STOP
www.nickscomedystop.com
A well-loved Theater District comedy club with local stars and would-be stars on stage.
✚ J6 ✉ 100 Warrenton Street ☎ 617/423-2900
🕐 Shows generally Thu 8.30, Fri, Sat 8.45 🚇 Boylston

OM BAR
Tucked in a former bank vault beneath Mantra restaurant, this bar's techno music and plush decor are as chilled as its martinis.
✚ J5 ✉ 52 Temple Plaza
☎ 617/542-8111
🚇 Park Street, Downtown Crossing

CHEAP THEATER
Prices for productions in the Theater District can be expensive. If you are willing to roll the dice, many college theater groups offer fine productions at lower prices. For example, the **Playwright's Theatre** at Boston University (949 Commonwealth Ave., 617-358-7529) showcases plays written or produced by students or alumni. Particularly popular is the annual **Boston Theater Marathon**, which features 50 10-minute plays every spring.

THE ROXY
www.roxyboston.com
Favored by international students, this dance club fills a beautifully converted former ballroom. On Friday, Chippendale dancers perform.
✚ J6 ✉ 287 Tremont Street
☎ 617/338-7699
🚇 Boylston, Chinatown

SILVERTONE BAR & GRILL
Popular subterranean joint just off the Common features comfy booths, creative martinis, and a bar menu of comfort food like mac 'n' cheese and meatloaf. Crowded on weekends.
✚ K5 ✉ 69 Bromfield Street
☎ 617/338-7887
🚇 Park Street

THE WANG THEATRE
www.citicenter.org
A 1920s movie palace used for concerts, opera, dance and the impressive Boston Ballet (tel 617/ 695-6950), which performs classical and contemporary dance. The 3,600-seat theater has undergone a renovation.
✚ J6 ✉ 270 Tremont Street
☎ 617/ 482-9393
🚇 Boylston

Restaurants

PRICES

Prices are approximate, based on a 3-course meal for one person.

$$$	over $40
$$	$20–$40
$	under $20

AUJOURD'HUI ($$$)
www.fourseasons.com/boston/dining
Overlooking the Public Garden and known as much for the service as the food, this is one of Boston's best formal restaurants. The chef's complex presentations and unusual combinations are pricey, but it's close to perfect.
J6 ✉ Four Seasons Hotel (▷ 112), 200 Boylston Street ☎ 617/351-2037 Dinner daily; brunch Sun Arlington

AURA ($$$)
www.seaportboston.com
Beautiful presentations that spotlight the inventive combinations of ingredients are the signature of Aura's imaginative chef. And the hotel's no-tipping policy applies here, too, making the prices less onerous than other restaurants of its high caliber. Desserts are outstanding.
L6 ✉ Seaport Hotel, 1 Seaport Lane (Northern Avenue) ☎ 617/385-4300 Dinner daily World Trade Center

BARKING CRAB ($)
A rough-and-ready clam shack where you can eat indoors or alfresco, with downtown views across the water. Expect crowds, a wait, noise and fun.
L6 ✉ 88 Sleeper Street, off Northern Avenue, Waterfront ☎ 617/426-2722 From 11.30am South Station

CAFÉ FLEURI ($$)
Bright and open, with well-spaced tables, this smart atrium café specializes in dishes created to showcase seasonal local ingredients. The Saturday Chocolate Bar is a decadent buffet of chocolate desserts.
K5 ✉ The Langham Boston, 250 Franklin Street ☎ 617/956-8751 Breakfast, lunch and dinner daily Downtown Crossing

PEOPLE-WATCHING
Some of the best restaurants are also the sites of its best people-watching scenes. On Boston Common, eateries like Excelsior and Via Matta invite you to survey the weekend strolls taken by crowds in the verdant Public Garden. In the South End, colorful hordes of people walk the sidewalks outside bistros like Hamersley's and Union Bar & Grille. But for the most eclectic sightings, go to Newbury Street, where the outdoor cafés are perfectly perched.

EXCELSIOR ($$$)
Many dishes at this luxurious, pricey restaurant overlooking the Public Garden feature unusual twists. Excellent lobster, lamb and steak entrees are some of the standouts on the Contemporary American menu.
H6 ✉ 227 Boylston Street, Theater District ☎ 617/426-7878 Lunch Mon–Fri; dinner daily Arlington

GINZA ($$)
www.ginzaboston.com
Easily some of the best raw fish in the city, Ginza is a magnet for sushi fanatics and Boston's late-night crowds. Don't miss the house specialty, spider *maki* (featuring tempura soft shell crab that resembles an arachnid).
J6 ✉ 16 Hudson Street ☎ 617/338-2261 Chinatown

GRILL 23 & BAR ($$$)
www.grill23.com
Steaks, prime rib of beef, lamb chops, swordfish and more. Attentive service in a men's club-style room.
H6 ✉ 161 Berkeley Street (at Stuart Street) ☎ 617/542-2255 Dinner daily Arlington

INTRIGUE CAFÉ ($)
Boston Harbor Hotel's waterside bar-restaurant and patio is one of the town's finest casual options—for both its top-notch shrimp cocktail and

its breezy, flower-festooned outdoor patio.
L5 ✉ 70 Rowes Wharf
☎ 617/439-7000
🚇 Aquarium

JUMBO SEAFOOD ($)

www.jumboseafoodrestaurant.com

Crowds flock to this enclave of superlative Chinese food for the superfresh, water tank-straight-to-wok shrimp, lobster and flounder dishes. Try giant clams in black-bean sauce
J6 ✉ 7 Hudson Street
☎ 617/542-2823
🚇 Chinatown

LEGAL TEST KITCHEN ($$)

A modern and daring offshoot of the Legal Sea Foods chain, this outpost serves up crunchy, cornmeal-fried clams and spicy Asian lobster. Ask to borrow one of the iPod docks on offer and you can have your own personal jukebox at your table.
L6 ✉ 225 Northern Avenue ☎ 617/330-7450
🚇 South Station

MERITAGE ($$$)

www.meritagetherestaurant.com

A feast for the eyes as well as the palate, dining at Meritage combines a quartet of superlatives: cuisine, wine pairings, service and harbor view.
L5 ✉ 70 Rowes Wharf
☎ 617/439-3995
🚇 Aquarium

NEW SHANGHAI ($)

www.newshanghaiboston.com

Upscale Chinatown eatery, specializing in Shanghai-style cuisine. Cold appetizers such as eggplant with garlic sauce.
J6 ✉ 21 Hudson Street
☎ 617/338-6688 🕐 Lunch, dinner 🚇 Chinatown

PEKING TOM'S LONGTANG LOUNGE ($$)

www.pekingtom.com

This place combines a hopping bar scene with a menu ranging from traditional Cantonese fare to sushi and Chinese-inspired nibbles.
K6 ✉ 25 Kingston Street, Downtown ☎ 617/482-6282
🕐 Lunch Sun–Fri, dinner daily
🚇 Downtown Crossing

RADIUS ($$$)

www.radiusrestaurant.com

Culinary hot spot set in a

1920s one-time bank. Chef Michael Schlow serves modern French cuisine: roasted halibut with cauliflower puree and lentils, venison in green peppercorn sauce.
K6 ✉ 8 High Street, Financial District
☎ 617/426-1234
🕐 Lunch Mon–Fri, dinner Mon–Sat 🚇 South Station

SEL DE LA TERRE ($$$)

www.seldelaterre.com

Across the street from the Aquarium, this Provençal spot offers simple, delicious bistro dishes. Try not to fill up on the superb bread.
K5 ✉ 255 State Street, Waterfront ☎ 617/720-1300
🕐 Lunch Mon–Fri,; dinner daily, brunch Sat, Sun, Wed–Sat late-night menu at the bar 🚇 South Station

TEATRO ($$–$$$)

www.teatroboston.com

A beautiful, blue-lit boite filled with theater-going crowds in for the authentic Italian menu.
J6 ✉ 177 Tremont Street, Downtown ☎ 617/778-6841
🕐 Dinner daily
🚇 Park Street

VIA MATTA ($$)

www.viamattarestaurant.com

Step into this chic, noisy dining room for simple but extremely fresh Italian specialties. In warm weather, make for the pretty, patio dining area.
H6 ✉ 79 Park Plaza
☎ 617/422-0014 🚇 Arlington

Back Bay and the South End

Home to some of the finest shopping and people-watching in all the city, Back Bay and the South End are also vibrant residential neighborhoods.

5

Charles   River   Basin

HARVARD   BRIDGE

2A

JAMES   J   STORROW
Back
BEACON
Street
Gloucester
Fairfield
St

6

Back   Street
Bay   State   Road
Marl-   borough
MASSACHUSETTS
BACK   BAY
COMMONWEALTH
Street
NEWBURY

Deerfield
Street
Kenmore
HEREFORD
STREET

KENMORE   COMMONWEALTH   AVENUE
SQUARE

Newbury   Street
Hynes
Convention
Center
BOYLSTON

BROOKLINE   AVENUE
MASSACHUSETTS   TURNPIKE   90
Newbury   Street
P
DALTON   ST

Prudential
Skywalk

Landsdowne   Street   Street
Ipswich   Street
Hynes
Convention
Center
BELVIDERE
STREET

Fenway   Park
Boston
Red Sox
Ipswich
AVENUE
Haviland St
Edgerley
Road
St Germain Street
Clearway
Street
BOYLSTON   STREET

7

Van   Ness   Street
Norway   St
New Edgerley
Rd
First Church of Christ
Scientist and
The Mapparium

Jersey   Street
DRIVE
Fens
FENWAY
Burbank   Street
Symphony

Peterborough   Street
Street
WESTLAND   AVENUE

Kilmarnock
Queensberry   Street
Agassiz   Road
Symphony   Street
STREET

HEMENWAY

PARK   BAY
Gainsborough
Street
HUNTINGTON

Back
Muddy   River
Stephen
Botolph

8

Spear St
Massachusetts
Avenue
Street

FENWAY
Forsyth   Way
Northeastern
University

Isabella Stewart
Gardner Museum
Museum of
Fine Arts
AVENUE
Greenleaf St
Camden
AVENUE
Carter
Pig

Palace Road
LOUIS PRANG ST
Museum Rd
STREET
Forsyth
STREET
Davenport
Burke St
Coventry
Lenox

Evans Way
HUNTINGTON
Museum of
Fine Arts
Tavern Road
Leon   Street
Cunard St
Benton St
Hammond St
Kendall Street

Tetlow
St
Evans Way
9
Field Street
Warwick
Greenwich
St

9
Vancouver
St
RUGGLES   STREET
PARKER   STREET
Ruggles
28
COLUMBUS
TREMONT
Windsor Street

0   250 m
0   250 yds

D   E   F

Charles River Esplanade

EMBANKMENT ROAD

Charles River Embankment
Storrow Lagoon

MEMORIAL DRIVE 1

Street

STREET

EXETER

Marlborough

Commonwealth

AVENUE

STREET

DARTMOUTH STREET

Street

2

BERKELEY

CLARENDON STREET

STREET

Gibson House Museum

Copley Theater

Newbury Street

STREET

Trinity Church and Copley Square

Copley

Boston Public Library

Prudential Center

Providence Street

AVENUE

JAMES ST

Hancock Tower

Lyric Stage

Street

Stuart

Back Bay/ South End

BERKELEY

CLARENDON

AVENUE

28

9

i

Harcourt St

Prudential

Garrison

Carlton

AVENUE

P

BACK BAY STATION

DARTMOUTH

COLUMBUS

CHANDLER STREET

STREET

Lawrence St

Street

Yarmouth Street

West

Holyoke

Braddock Parkway

NEWTON

Appleton

Gray Street

Warren

Street

Gray Street

Avenue Boston Center for the Arts

Dwight Street

Milford Street

Durham Street

W.

Rutland Squares

AVENUE

Canton Avenue

Warren Avenue

Montgomery St

TREMONT STREET

Hanson Street

Union Pk

Waltham

Street

Bradford St

GREENWICH PKWY

Clearmont Pk

COLUMBUS

CONCORD SQUARE

Springfield

Worcester

WEST CONCORD

Pembroke Street

West Brookline Street

STREET

Rutland Street

DEDHAM STREET

SHAWMUT

Upton Street

AVENUE

Union Street

Park

STREET

MONS REYNOLDS WAY

MALDEN ST

Plympton Street

MASSACHUSETTS

TREMONT

STREET

Rutland Street

AVENUE

STREET

Blackstone Square

WASHINGTON

SOUTH END

Franklin Square

St George

HARRISON

Wareham Street

Northampton

Street

SHAWMUT

AVENUE

WASHINGTON

EAST CONCORD

Worcester Square

STREET

East Newton

East Brookline Street

EAST NEWTON

AVENUE

St

E Dedham Street

E Canton Street

STREET

STREET

ALBANY

Ramsey Park

G

HARRISON STREET

H

Boston Public Library

The illuminated marble staircase (left) and cloisters (below)

HIGHLIGHTS

● Puvis de Chavannes murals
● John Singer Sargent murals
● Daniel Chester French bronze doors
● The courtyard

TIP

● Free films are screened regularly in the Raab Lecture Hall.

This is no ordinary library. Behind its granite facade lies an opulent institution built in Renaissance palazzo style and decorated with sculptures and paintings by some of the best artists of the day.

The education of the people A people's palace dedicated to the advancement of learning was what Charles Follen McKim was commissioned to design. An architectural landmark in the classical style, facing H. H. Richardson's Romanesque Trinity Church across Copley Square, it opened its doors to the public in 1895. It is now the Research Library, the General Library being housed in the adjoining 1972 Johnson Building.

Further treasures Pass between Bela Pratt's voluptuous bronzes, *Science* and *Art* (1912), to enter through Daniel Chester French's bronze doors. Ascend the marble staircase, guarded by lions by Louis Saint-Gaudens (Augustus's brother), and from its windows catch a glimpse of the peaceful courtyard. The stairs and landing are decorated with panels by Puvis de Chavannes, whimsical representations of the muses of inspiration. The Abbey Room has paintings depicting the quest for the Holy Grail, by Edwin Austin Abbey. Bates Hall is a magnificent room; get a close-up view of its highly decorative, barrel-vaulted ceiling from the stairs that lead up to the Sargent Gallery. The John Singer Sargent murals, *Triumph of Religion*, completed in 1919, were restored in 2004. Pause to sit in the colonnaded courtyard, watching the fountain and enjoying the tranquillity.

Commonwealth Avenue

A Parisian-style boulevard lined with the grandest houses in Boston is at the heart of an amazing piece of 19th-century urban planning. To walk down it is to be transported to a different age.

Landfill By the 1850s, Boston was getting over-crowded. Desperate for land, developers turned to the swampy "back bay" of the Charles River, embarking on a remarkable landfill project to create a new residential district. Inspired by Paris's boulevard system, the architect Arthur Gilman planned a grid, eight blocks long and four blocks wide, with a long central mall.

Commonwealth Avenue Even the *nouveau-riche* industrialists who flocked to the Back Bay felt some of the Puritan restraints of the Proper Bostonians of Beacon Hill, and their rows of ostentatious brownstones are a somewhat subdued blend of Victorian styles. The centerpiece is Commonwealth Avenue. Central gardens are lined with trees; in spring magnolias bloom in profusion. The Boston Women's Memorial lies between Fairfield and Gloucester streets. Most houses are now apartments, some are offices. The châteaulike Burrage Mansion at Hereford Street stands out, with statuettes everywhere. To see inside a more average home, visit Gibson House Museum on Beacon Street.

Feeling fit? The mall is just part of a 7-mile long (11km) "Emerald Necklace" of green space stretching from Boston Common to Franklin Park.

THE BASICS

➕ G6
🚇 Newbury and Boylston streets
Ⓣ Arlington, Copley, Hynes Convention Center

HIGHLIGHTS

● Magnolias in spring on Commonwealth Avenue
● Lights on the mall at Christmas
● Memorial to firemen killed in Hotel Vendome fire

TIPS

● More intimate than Commonwealth Avenue and no less beautiful is next-door Marlborough Street, which is lined with flowering dogwoods in the springtime.
● North–south streets are named alphabetically, Arlington to Hereford.

Isabella Stewart Gardner Museum

The woman who created this collection of "beautiful things" had a passion for art, music and horticulture. Her finds are arranged in a Venetian-style house built around a flower-filled courtyard.

"Beautiful things" Determined to give her country "beautiful things," Mrs Gardner made a start in 1896 by buying a Rembrandt self-portrait. Her collection grew to include work by Vermeer, Giotto, Botticelli, Raphael, Degas and Matisse, as well as John Singer Sargent and James McNeill Whistler. She also bought prints and drawings, books, sculptures, ceramics and glass, tapestries, carpets, lace, stained glass, ironwork and furniture.

Music and horticulture The building itself, known as Fenway Court, and the atmosphere

Looking down at the Venetian-style courtyard of the Isabella Stewart Gardner Museum (left); the interior facade that overlooks the courtyard, which is filled with planting and statuary (below)

that pervades it, is as much the creation of Mrs Gardner as her collection. She arranged her objects in a series of rooms—the Raphael Room, the Titian Room, the Gothic Room, the intimate Blue Room and more. She filled the courtyard with sculptures, plants and trees, and she celebrated the opening of her home (she lived on the top floor) to the public with a concert given by members of the Boston Symphony Orchestra. Today, concerts are held in the Tapestry Room on winter weekends.

Art heist The collection suffered a terrible loss—and America's biggest art theft—in March 1990 when thieves dressed as policemen made off with 13 items, which have not been recovered. Among them were a priceless Vermeer and *The Sea of Galilee*, Rembrandt's only seascape.

THE BASICS

www.gardnermuseum.org
✚ D8
✉ 280 The Fenway
☎ 617/566-1401
🕐 Tue–Sun 11–5.
Closed Mon except most public hols
🍴 On premises
Ⓜ Museum
(Green line E)
♿ Good
✋ Expensive. Boston CityPass applies
❓ Concerts: Sep–Apr Sat, Sun 1.30 ☎ 617/734-1359. Tour: Fri 2.30. Courtyard: talks most weekdays (times posted at the information desk). Lectures, shop

Museum of Fine Arts

HIGHLIGHTS

- Nubian collection
- Impressionist room
- Copley portraits
- Tang dynasty earthenware

TIPS

- Every Friday night, the MFA breaks out wine and jazz for a refined singles scene.
- Tickets to the museum are good for another visit within a week, so you can catch the art you missed!
- The Children's Room for those age 6–12 has hands-on projects.

The MFA is one of America's foremost museums. The Asian collection is unrivaled in this hemisphere, the European art is superb, the American rooms excellent. If time is limited, take a guided tour of the highlights.

Asian, Egyptian, Classical The MFA's Nubian collection is the best outside the Sudan. It is all exquisite, from the neat rows of little *shawabtis* (figurines) to the faience jewelry. The Egyptian rooms are popular, with mummies, hieroglyphics and splendid Old Kingdom sculptures. Buddhist sculptures, Chinese ceramics and Indian paintings make up part of an Asian collection.

European In the Evans Wing upstairs, seek out the little gem of a Rembrandt in a glass case, then

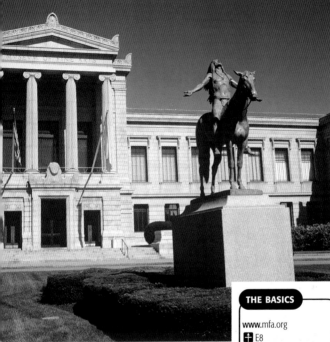

A lofty corridor in the museum (below left); Cyrus Dallin's 1909 statue Appeal to the Great Spirit *stands at the entrance to the museum (below)*

take in works of Tiepolo, Gainsborough, Turner, Delacroix, Constable and a good number of Millets. The Impressionist room is an array of familiar paintings, with works from Monet and Renoir to Gauguin. There is porcelain from all over Europe and period rooms from Britain.

American New England furniture and decorative arts feature in a series of period rooms. Near the silver is a fine musical instruments collection. As for the art of New England, downstairs in the Evans Wing, begin with the Copley portraits, work through the 19th-century landscape painters Fitz Hugh Lane and Thomas Cole, and move on to John Singer Sargent, and, from the 20th century, Childe Hassam, Edward Hopper and Lilian Westacott Hale. In the Contemporary Art room find works by Georgia O'Keeffe and Stuart Davis.

THE BASICS

www.mfa.org
➕ E8
✉ 465 Huntington Avenue
☎ 617/267-9300
🕐 Mon, Tue 10–4.45, Wed–Fri 10–9.45 (Thu, Fri after 5, Evans Wing and selected galleries only), Sat, Sun 10–4.45
🍴 Choice on premises
Ⓜ Museum (Greenline E)
♿ Excellent
💲 Expensive. Wed 4–9.45 voluntary contribution. Boston CityPass applies
❓ Guided walks Mon–Sat. Tea and Music Tue–Fri 2.30–4. Lectures, films, concerts. Good shop

Newbury Street

TOP 25

Newbury Street houses
retail and residential
buildings (below and
below left)

THE BASICS

www.newbury-st.com

⊞ G6

✉ Between Arlington
Street and Massachusetts
Avenue

🕐 Most shops open 10–6

🍴 Excellent bistros line
each side of the street

🚇 Arlington, Copley
Massachusetts Avenue

♿ Fair to excellent,
depending on the business.
Many have elevators

HIGHLIGHTS

● Window-shopping in
Newbury Street
● People-watching in the
Newbury Street cafés
● Newbury Street trompe
l'oeil murals at Boston
Architectural Center and
No. 354.

**Newbury Street is the place to go if you
are interested in buying artwork—
paintings, prints or sculpture. But art
isn't the only draw at Boston's answer
to Paris's Champs-Élysées.**

Galleries Many a pleasant hour can be spent
browsing in the galleries, stopping off in a café
now and then. Individual small shops are housed
in beautiful historic rowhouses (terraces). A
concentration of galleries lies between Arlington
and Exeter streets. They display works by
18th- and 19th-century artists, in addition to
contemporary pieces. The Robert Klein Gallery, at
38 Newbury Street, is the only major art gallery in
New England dedicated to fine art photography. If
you are interested in avant-garde galleries explore
the South End, particularly around Harrison and
Thayer streets.

Shop, shop, shop Shopping is also an enormous
draw of the area. At the intersection with Arlington
Street, where shops tend to be high-end and high-
priced, shoppers find plenty of international
jewelry shops, fashion designers and day spas.
That stable gives way to more mid-range shops
as you move toward the other end of the street,
which intersects with Massachusetts Avenue. On
the way there, cross mainstream fashion chains,
gift shops, independent boutiques and hair salons.
One thing the entire street lays claim to, however,
is an abundance of cafés and restaurants. Duck
into any with an outdoor patio to get a first-rate
spot for people-watching.

Prudential Center and Skywalk

The view from the tower at night (below); retail outlets (below right)

An architecturally unremarkable building offering bird's-eye views of Boston and the New England countryside from its 50th floor. Drop back closer to the ground for shops and eating places.

Skywalk at the Prudential Tower The Prudential Tower is architecturally undistinguished, part of the 1960s Prudential Center office and shopping complex. But take the elevator to the Skywalk on the 50th floor and you have stunning 360-degree views—weather permitting, as far as the mountains of New Hampshire. Pick out the gold dome of the State House; peer down onto the rooftops of the neat Back Bay homes and over the Charles River to MIT and Cambridge; see the parks of the "Emerald Necklace" stretching into the distance; look out to the Boston Harbor Islands. Interactive exhibits cover key historical and sporting events, as well as distinguished buildings and residents. Looking to relax while soaking up that same stunning view? The Top of the Hub restaurant, on the Pru's 52nd floor, looks out to the twinkling city and beyond; be sure to stop in for a cocktail or dessert, and a city profile you won't soon forget.

Down to earth Meanwhile, on the lower levels of the building, find plenty of indoor shopping and snacking. The food courtyard caters to diners-in-a-rush with chain cafés (some healthy, some not) and several more sedate sit-down establishments, while the stores lure shoppers in for high-end jewelry, international fashions, quality stationery and even flowers.

THE BASICS

www.prudentialcenter.com

➕ G7

✉ Prudential Tower, 800 Boylston Street

☎ 617/859-0648

🕐 Daily 10–10. Skywalk: Mar–end Oct 10–9.30, Nov–end Feb 10–8

🍴 Top of the Hub; choice in Prudential Center

🚇 Prudential, Hynes Convention Center

♿ Excellent

💰 Expensive. Boston CityPass applies

HIGHLIGHTS

● Views from the Pru after snow
● Views from the Pru at night
● Top of the Hub bar and restaurant on the 52nd floor
● Sushi at Haru, outside the Huntington Avenue entrance
● Crane Stationery for top-quality cards and papers

The South End

First occupied by musicians and teachers in the 1850s, the South End had taken a social nose-dive by the end of the 19th century but is now very much back in vogue with young professionals and artists.

Residential It is a lively residential area, whose elegant bow-fronted terraces, many profusely decorated with balustrades and window boxes, line leafy streets and squares. Running through the middle is Tremont Street, where local shops are punctuated by trendy places to eat. There is a broad ethnic mix here and a strong gay community. The South End has a growing number of art galleries, particularly around Harrison and Thayer streets. The neighborhood lies between Huntington Avenue and the Expressway.

The South End's Victorian houses (left and below)

So Wa'? The most rapidly changing area of the South End, however, is the SoWa district (named such because it sits South of Washington Street). Blessed with the hottest new restaurants and cafés—from Union Bar & Grille to Flour Bakery (both ▷ 84)—the area currently has some of the most expensive real estate and most adventurous interior design in the city, but it has still not been entirely gentrified, (a fact that locals say lends it an urbane, gritty feel).

By day and by night Walk the neighborhood's parks during the day, admire its rooftops and the tiny gardens in front of its brownstones, visit its trendy art galleries and home goods shops, then stay to enjoy dinner in its stylish restaurants. Spring and summer bring elaborate gardens into bloom and fine alfresco dining.

THE BASICS

www.southend.org
✚ H8
✉ Between the Expressway and Massachusetts Avenue
🕐 Most shops open 10–6. Most restaurants open 5pm–midnight
🍴 Excellent bistros line each side of the street
🚇 Back Bay/South End New England Medical Center
♿ Fair to excellent, depending on the business. Many have elevators

75

Trinity Church and Copley Square

HIGHLIGHTS

Trinity Church
- Polychrome interior
- John La Farge paintings and lancet windows
- Lantern tower
- Christmas candlelight services

TIP

- Lunchtime organ concerts every Friday at 12.15 take advantage of Trinity Church's exceptional acoustics.

H. H. Richardson's prototype French Romanesque church is often described as America's masterpiece of ecclesiastical architecture. It faces Copley Square, bounded by other notable buildings—Boston Public Library and the Fairmont Copley Plaza Hotel.

Trinity Church The Back Bay was a newly developed landfill area when in 1872 Henry Hobson Richardson was commissioned to draw up designs for a new Trinity Church. A massive lantern tower over the transept crossing dominates the church inside and out, requiring more than 2,000 wooden piles massed together to support its granite foundations. Externally, the granite blocks are broken up by bands of pink sandstone. Inside, John La Farge created an intricate polychrome interior, a

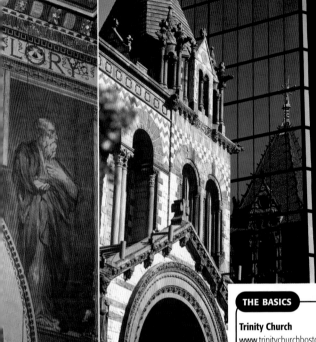

Trinity Church sits alongside its tall neighbor, reflected in the mirrorlike glass (left); detail of the ornate frescos by John La Farge that decorate the walls above the gilded archway in Trinity Church (middle); the contrast of 19th-century and 20th-century architecture (right)

tapestry of reds and greens highlighted with gold. The church also contains several important examples of La Farge's ground-breaking stained-glass work. In the baptistery is a bust by Daniel Chester French of the portly rector Phillips Brooks, who composed the carol "O Little Town of Bethlehem."

John Hancock Tower There is something immensely serene about this icy shaft of blue glass. Designed by Henry Cobb, of I. M. Pei & Partners, the building caused a big sensation at first. But it has long since found a place in (most) Bostonians' hearts. After 9/11, the observatory on the 60th floor was closed to the public, for security reasons. But visitors can still admire the tower from the outside, walking around it to see how clearly it reflects the historic buildings around it.

THE BASICS

Trinity Church
www.trinitychurchboston.
org
✚ G6
✉ Copley Square
☎ 617/536-0944
🕐 Daily 8–6
Ⓟ Copley
♿ Good
🖐 Free
❓ Free half-hour organ recitals Fri 12.15. Sun services 8, 9, 11 (with choir music), 6

John Hancock Tower
✚ H6
✉ Copley Square
🍴 Nearby
Ⓟ Copley

More to See

BACK BAY FENS

Once a saltwater bay, this was the first of Frederick Law Olmsted's string of parks, part of the so-called "Emerald Necklace" of open green spaces. Tall rushes line the banks of the Muddy River behind the Museum of Fine Arts; stroll through the willows or sit in the Rose Garden.

🕂 E8 ✉ The Fenway/Park Drive
🚇 Museum, Hynes Convention Center

CHARLES RIVER ESPLANADE

A favorite for roller blading, jogging, sunbathing, boating and biking. Free summer concerts in Hatch Shell (▷ 82). Also open-air film screenings. Boat tours leave from near the Science Museum.

🕂 H5 ✉ Storrow Memorial Drive
🚇 Charles/MGH

FENWAY PARK FOR RED SOX

www.redsox.com

The Boston Red Sox play from April through October. "Friendly Fenway," famous for its Green Monster, the high left-field wall, is the oldest ballpark in the US. Renovations include new seating and a food concourse.

🕂 E7 ✉ 24 Yawkey Way ☎ Tickets: 617/267-1700 or Ticketmaster 617/931-2000. Tours: 617/236-6666 🚇 Kenmore Square

FIRST CHURCH OF CHRIST, SCIENTIST AND THE MAPPARIUM

www.tfccs.com

The scale of this complex is mind-blowing. The world headquarters for the Church of Christ, Scientist, occupies 4 acres (6ha) of prime Back Bay land, with a church seating 3,000. The Mother Church of Christian Science was founded in Boston in 1892 by Mary Baker Eddy. The Mapparium, on the first floor of the Mary Baker Eddy Library, is a brightly colored stained-glass globe, so huge you can walk inside it and stand at the center of the world. It was made in the early 1930s. Try out the echo to get decidedly weird effects.

🕂 F7 ✉ 175 Huntington Avenue; Library: 200 Massachusetts Avenue ☎ 617/450-2000
🕐 Daily; Library Tue–Sun 10–4
🚇 Prudential 🎫 Library: moderate

A floodlighted Red Sox baseball game at Fenway Park

South End Stroll

You will see Victorian architecture, boutiques, restaurants and parks. Make sure you leave time to stop, browse and snack.

DISTANCE: 1.6 miles (2.5km) **ALLOW:** 3–6 hours

START
➕ G7 🚇 Back Bay

DARTMOUTH STREET

① From Back Bay Station, walk several blocks down Dartmouth Street, crossing Columbus Avenue, noting the brick sidewalks and brownstone buildings on Chandler and Appleton streets.

② Continue down Dartmouth to Tremont Street, on the right are the Boston Center for the Arts (▷ 82), and local institution Hamersley's Bistro (▷ 84).

③ Across Tremont, find much-loved restaurants such as B&G Oyster and the Butcher Shop.

④ From the Butcher Shop, take a left down Tremont and pass gift shops and bistros such as Aquitaine and Metropolis.

END
➕ F8 🚇 Massachusetts Avenue

MASSACHUSETTS AVENUE

⑧ Walk three blocks past Columbus Avenue and follow South End mall, a flower-filled walkway to the left until it meets Massachusetts Avenue.

⑦ You're now in the South End's trendiest section, full of new restaurants, galleries and stores. Take a right on Washington, passing restaurants like Union Bar & Grille (▷ 84), and stores like Lekker (▷ 80). Next take a right on West Concord Street.

⑥ Continue down West Brookline, passing Blackstone Square, a small neighborhood park. When you reach Washington Street, take a left.

⑤ Where Tremont crosses West Brookline Street, take a left.

Shopping

ALAN BILZERIAN
A fun one for window-shopping (or buying, of course, if you're very rich or very outrageous) for the latest from Jean-Paul Gaultier, Katharine Hamnett and the like.
H6 ⊠ 34 Newbury Street
☎ 617/536-1001
Ⓣ Arlington

ALLEN EDMONDS
Top-quality shoes in classic styles come in an impressively wide range of sizes.
H6 ⊠ 36 Newbury Street
☎ 617/247-3363
Ⓣ Arlington

ARTFUL HAND
American crafts, including woven silk scarfs, woodwork, ceramics and glass. In Copley Place Mall.
G7 ⊠ 36 Copley Place
☎ 617/262-9601
Ⓣ Copley, Prudential

BARNEYS NEW YORK
A second home to the city's high-spending hipsters, where you can find of-the-moment labels like 3.1 by Philip Lim and Lanvin. Don't miss the luxurious shoe section anchored by a fireplace.
G7 ⊠ 100 Huntington Avenue Ⓣ 617/385-3300
Ⓣ Copley

BROOKSTONE
Household, personal and travel equipment here goes well beyond the definition of "gadgets"– useful, high-quality tools for living that you never

knew existed.
G7 ⊠ Copley Place
☎ 617/567-7641 Ⓣ Copley

COPLEY FLAIR
A full stable of stationery and cards, plus novelty pens, gift wrap, and assorted other specialty gifts for every holiday.
G6 ⊠ 583 Boylston Street
☎ 617/247-1648 Ⓣ Copley

EMPORIO ARMANI
Slightly less haute couture but more accessible price-wise than Giorgio Armani (No. 22 Newbury Street). The store has a popular café, with outside tables in summer—just the place after some serious shopping.
G6 ⊠ 2 Copley Place
☎ 617/262-7300 Ⓣ Copley

FILENE'S BASEMENT
With little in common (except the crowded

MORE CHOICE

These large outdoor activity stores are all on Commonwealth Avenue.

Eastern Mountain Sports
Hiking, backpacking, camping, mountaineering, cross-country skiing.
⊠ 1041 Commonwealth Avenue ☎ 617/254-4250

Ski Market
Skiing, snowboarding, in-line skating, biking. Ski and snowboard rentals. Good children's section.
⊠ 860 Commonwealth Avenue ☎ 617/731-6100

racks and narrow aisles) with the beloved old "real" basement at Downtown Crossing, this new incarnation sells off-price high-price without the great values and automatic markdowns that made the old store fun.
G6 ⊠ 497 Boylston Street
☎ 617/424-5520 Ⓣ Copley

GRETTALUXE
Find pretty, hard-to-find designs by posh global designers (Barbara Bui and Missoni to Chloe) for women, plus chic (and très chère) handbags and shoes.
G7 ⊠ 10 Huntington Avenue Ⓣ 617/536-1959
Ⓣ Copley

LEKKER
"Lekker" is a Dutch word meaning alluring and attractive. This South End store sells unique European home accessories and furniture.
G9 ⊠ 1317 Washington Street ☎ 617/542-6464
Ⓣ Union Park Street

LUSH
This shop bursts with fragrance and friendliness, as well as with vibrant color. Handmade soaps and other earth-kind cosmetics are bright, unusual, nicely packaged and reasonably priced. These make good easy-to-pack gifts.
G6 ⊠ 166 Newbury Street
☎ 617/375-5874 Ⓣ Copley

SHOPPING

BACK BAY AND THE SOUTH END

MARC JACOBS
The celebrated American designer showcases both his more expensive and casual lines at this funky but posh boutique. Duck in to find women's coats, dresses, pants (trousers) and skirts, plus accessories and home decor.
➕ G6 ✉ 81 Newbury Street
☎ 617/425-0707 🚇 Copley

MATSU
Chic gifts and (a few) clothes, many Asian.
➕ G6 ✉ 259 Newbury Street ☎ 617/266-9707
🚇 Copley, Hynes Convention Center

NEWBURY COMICS
The hippest record shop in town. CDs, T-shirts, posters and comics.
➕ G6 ✉ 332 Newbury Street
☎ 617/236-4930
🚇 Hynes Convention Center

NIKETOWN
Large, state-of-the-art store, arranged by pavilion: men's and women's shoes for training and running, golf, basketball, soccer, tennis and more.
➕ G6 ✉ 200 Newbury Street
☎ 617/267-3400 🚇 Copley

PIERRE DEUX
French fabrics, wallpapers, table linens and lampshades.
➕ G6 ✉ 111 Newbury Street
☎ 617/536-6364
🚇 Arlington

POTTERY BARN
Stylish accessories and furniture.

➕ G6 ✉ 122 Newbury Street ☎ 617/266-6553
🚇 Arlington

PRUDENTIAL CENTER
A dozen clothes stores (including Chico's, Ann Taylor, J. Jill and Olympia Sports), some shoe and accessories shops, gift and specialty (such as Crane's stationery) stores and a hardware store. Also home to department stores Saks Fifth Avenue and Lord & Taylor, a post office, ATMs, a superb food court and Legal Sea Foods.
➕ G7 ✉ Between Boylston Street and Huntington Avenue
🕐 Mon–Sat 10–9, Sun 11–6
🚇 Prudential

THE ROCKPORT STORE
Good quality and comfort in this excellent store. Sandals, boots, loafers

INDEPENDENT SHOPS

Amid Boston's many national and international chain stores, you'll find plenty of homegrown and family-run boutiques and specialty shops. How to best find them? When walking on Newbury Street, look up. The second, third, and fourth floors of the street's Victorian brownstone buildings are favorite spaces for those with less money to burn on front-and-center retail space, but with plenty of interesting and unique wares to peddle.

and walking shoes for all the family. You can get all your shoe accessories here.
➕ G6 ✉ 83 Newbury Street
☎ 617/421-1900 🚇 Arlington

SECOND TIME AROUND
Not your usual thrift shop, this resale shop specializes in better brands and higher quality. But it's more accessible than the traditional Junior League designer resale shops. You never know what you'll find here.
➕ G6 ✉ 176 Newbury Street
☎ 617/247-3504 🚇 Copley

SIMON PEARCE
Exquisite handmade art glass and utilitarian glassware beautiful enough to be decorator pieces. Simon Pearce is a well-known New England artist.
➕ G6 ✉ 115 Newbury Street
☎ 617/450-8388 🚇 Arlington

VIRGIN MEGASTORE
Loads of new music CDs, DVDs and other media, all packed into a multiple-floor emporium.
➕ H6 ✉ 360 Newbury Street
☎ 617/896-0950
🚇 Massachusetts Avenue

WILLIAMS-SONOMA
For the cook who has everything—or so you thought until you came in here: from Dualit toasters and heart-shaped muffin baking trays to French table linens.
➕ G7 ✉ Copley Place
☎ 617/262-5892 🚇 Copley

Entertainment and Nightlife

28 DEGREES
www.28degrees-boston.com
The chic South End lounge, known for its martinis, is next to the long-time favorite restaurant, Icarus. Tapas-style dishes are pricey, but you're paying for the scene and the vibe as much as for the food (which is good).
H7 ✉ 1 Appleton Street ☎ 617/728-0728 🚇 Back Bay/South End

BERKLEE PERFORMANCE CENTER
www.berkleebpc.com
This Back Bay venue seats 1,220 and hosts jazz, pop, folk and world music concerts by international performers and by the students and staff of the Berklee College of Music.
F7 ✉ 136 Massachusetts Avenue ☎ 617/266-7455 or 617/747-2261 🚇 Hynes Convention Center

BOSTON BILLIARD CLUB
www.bostonbilliardclub.com
Popular Fenway Park hangout for pool addicts.
F7 ✉ 126 Brookline Avenue ☎ 617/536-7665 🕐 Noon–2am 🚇 Kenmore

BOSTON CENTER FOR THE ARTS
www.bcaonline.org
Three stages at this South End performance space house several contemporary theater companies, including the Irish-theme Súgán Theatre and the cutting-edge SpeakEasy Stage Company.
H7 ✉ 539 Tremont Street ☎ 617/426-2787 🚇 Back Bay/South End

BOSTON PUBLIC LIBRARY
www.bpl.org
The occasional film series usually features lesser-known old films.
G7 ✉ Copley Square ☎ 617/536-5400 🚇 Copley

BUKOWSKI TAVERN
More than 100 varieties of suds are on offer at this friendly and unpretentious spot. The beer drinker in your group will be in heaven.
F7 ✉ 50 Dalton Street ☎ 617/437-9999 🚇 Hynes Convention Center

CASK 'N FLAGON
www.casknflagon.com
The perfect pit-stop before, during and after a Red Sox game, this rowdy

---

BLUE LAWS

The legacy of the Puritans continues in strict state laws to curtail imbibing. Most bars in Boston and Cambridge close at 1am during the week, and 2am on the weekends–though you may find restaurants in Chinatown that still serve later. Happy-hour specials, such as 2-for-1 drinks, are also prohibited, though some bars serve free appetizers after work.

---

sports bar has enough big-screen TVs to please the biggest fan.
D7 ✉ 62 Brookline Avenue ☎ 617/536-4840 🚇 Kenmore

CITY-BAR
www.citybarboston.com
Ultradim lighting and a stellar martini list makes this cool little hideaway inside the Lenox Hotel perfect for a mysterious rendezvous.
G6 ✉ 61 Exeter Street ☎ 617/933-4800 🚇 Copley, Back Bay/South End

CLUB CAFÉ
www.clubcafe.com
A nightly playground for the gay and lesbian crowd, this upscale lounge, restaurant and "video bar" literally has something—and somebody—for everyone.
H7 ✉ 209 Columbus Avenue ☎ 617/536-0966 🚇 Back Bay/South End

DELUX CAFE
Christmas lights, Elvis statues and Dr. Seuss wallpaper in the bathrooms. The interior here is as eclectic as its clientele. Try the tasty bar menu.
H7 ✉ 100 Chandler Street ☎ 617/338-5258 🚇 Back Bay

HATCH SHELL
www.state.ma.us/mdc
The Boston Pops Orchestra gives free concerts here in early July. The highlight is the concert with fireworks on

July 4 Other musical groups perform throughout the summer.
✠ H5 ✉ Esplanade, Embankment Road
☎ 617/727-1300
Ⓣ Charles/MGH, Arlington

HUNTINGTON THEATER COMPANY
www.bu.edu/huntington
Performances from Boston University's resident professional troupe include European and American, classical and modern, comedies and musicals.
✠ F7 ✉ 264 Huntington Avenue ☎ 617/266-0800
Ⓣ Symphony

JILLIAN'S
www.jilliansboston.com
Virtual sports, 200 high-tech games, 50 pool tables, plus five bars and bistro-style food.
✠ E7 ✉ 145 Ipswich Street
☎ 617/437-0300 Ⓓ Daily 11am–2am Ⓣ Kenmore

JORDAN HALL
www.newenglandconservatory.edu/ jordanhall/about.html
This glittering and acoustically perfect venue, in the prestigious New England Conservatory, showcases the resident Boston Philharmonic, Boston Baroque, and Cantata Singers. Conservatory students perform free concerts year-round.
✠ E8 ✉ 30 Gainsborough Street, one block west of Symphony Hall ☎ 617/585-1260 Ⓣ Symphony

KINGS
www.jkingsbackbay.com
This subterranean spot has the latest electronic scoring equipment. Relax in the hipster lounge after you tire of rolling strikes or gutter-balls.
✠ F7 ✉ 10 Scotia Street
☎ 617/266-2695
Ⓣ Hynes Convention Center

MUSEUM OF FINE ARTS
www.mfa.org/film/
International, early and offbeat films.
✠ E8 ✉ 465 Huntington Avenue ☎ 617/267-9300
Ⓣ Museum

STEVE SWEENEY'S COMEDY CAFÉ@JAE'S
The acerbic Boston comic sets the tone at this swank underground lounge.

PUPPETS

If your image of puppetry involves paper bags and pipe cleaners, you'll be amazed by the performances at the **Puppet Showplace Theatre** (32 Station Street, Brookline, 617/731-6400; www.puppetshowplace.org). Masters of pantomime spin yarns with surprisingly elaborate puppets that draw on traditions from around the world. In addition to weekly family shows, "puppets at night" performances and monthly "puppet slams" appeal to adult audiences.

✠ F7 ✉ 711 Boylston St.
☎ 800/401-2221 Ⓣ Copley

SYMPHONY HALL
www.bso.org
"Symphony" is home to the renowned Boston Symphony Orchestra from October through April. The orchestra performs on Friday afternoon, Saturday, Tuesday and Thursday evenings. Open rehearsals are held some Wednesday evenings and Thursday mornings. The Boston Pops Orchestra concerts are held here in May and June before moving to the Hatch Shell (▷ left) in July.
✠ F7 ✉ 301 Massachusetts Avenue ☎ Box office 617/266-1200; general information 617/266-1492 Ⓣ Symphony

TIKI ROOM
www.tikiroom.com
A rowdy spot before and after Red Sox games, this Polynesian-theme club draws sports fans and colleges kids for scorpion bowls, coconut mojitos, and… s'mores (marshmallow and chocolate between crackers).
✠ E7 ✉ 1 Landsdowne Street ☎ 617/351-2580
Ⓣ Kenmore

Restauants

PRICES

Prices are approximate, based on a 3-course meal for one person.

$$$	over $40
$$	$20–$40
$	under $20

BOMBOA ($$–$$$)

Don't let the trendy bar crowd keep you from finding a table here. A creative mix of French and Brazilian, the dishes—ceviche, feijoada or steak frites with chimichurri sauce—are very good.

➕ H7 ✉ 35 Stanhope Street ☎ 617/236-6363 🕐 Tue–Sat 5.30pm–midnight, Sun–Mon 5.30pm–10pm 🚇 Back Bay

BRASSERIE JO ($$–$$$)

www.brasseriejo.com
Opposite the Prudential Center, this traditional French brasserie specializes in Alsatian dishes, but serves all the French faves, from onion tart to coq au vin. Desserts are knockouts.

➕ G7 ✉ 120 Huntington Avenue ☎ 617/425-3240 🕐 Breakfast, lunch, dinner daily 🚇 Prudential

CLIO ($$$)

www.eliothotel.com
Excellent fare that's creative without being weird. The leopard-print rug adds just the right level of "chic." Good seafood preparations include chilled lobster and scallops with hot-and-sour bell-pepper broth. The sashimi bar is excellent.

➕ F6 ✉ Eliot Hotel, 370a Commonwealth Avenue, Back Bay ☎ 617/536-7200 🕐 Breakfast daily; dinner Tue–Sun 🚇 Hynes

FLOUR BAKERY ($)

www.flourbakery.com
Grab inexpensive, fast lunches and dinners (plus delicious pies, cakes and cookies) at this neighborhood favorite.

➕ H8 ✉ 1595 Washington Street ☎ 617/267-4300 🚇 Back Bay/South End

HAMERSLEY'S BISTRO ($$$)

www.hamersleybistro.com
Excellent American-French dishes; try roast chicken with garlic and lemon.

➕ H7 ✉ 553 Tremont Street (at Clarendon), South End ☎ 617/423-2700 🕐 Dinner daily 🚇 Back Bay/South End

HARU ($$)

www.harusushi.com
Sushi-and-sake-bar extraordinaire, this smartly styled restaurant offers not just exemplary sushi, but tempura that melts in the mouth and a sophisticated menu that includes favorites along with some inspired new creations.

➕ G7 ✉ 55 Huntington Avenue ☎ 617/536-0770 🚇 Prudential

ICARUS ($$$)

www.icarusrestaurant.com
Seasonal ingredients make up a sophisticated menu that might include chestnut-stuffed pork or ribeye in sour-cherry port sauce. Three-course chef's tasting menus are a good value.

➕ H7 ✉ 3 Appleton Street, South End ☎ 617/426-1790 🕐 Dinner daily 🚇 Back Bay/South End

L'ESPALIER ($$$)

www.lespalier.com
Superb contemporary fare in the formal setting of a 19th-century Back Bay house. Prix fixe.

➕ F6 ✉ 30 Gloucester Street, Back Bay ☎ 617/262-3023 🕐 Dinner Mon–Sat; tea Sat, Sun 🚇 Hynes Convention Center

PETIT ROBERT BISTRO ($$)

www.petitrobertbistro.com
A bistro in the truest Parisian sense, serving serious foods at sensible prices. Look for unusual ingredients, mouthwatering patés and perfectly seared foie gras. After dinner sit at the downstairs dessert bar to watch the pastry chef create your dessert.

➕ E6 ✉ 468 Commonwealth Avenue ☎ 617/375-0699 🚇 Kenmore

UNION BAR & GRILLE ($$)

www.unionrestaurant.com
Stylish and often packed bar/restaurant, serving big plates of burgers and house-cured duck confit.

➕ Off map at G9 ✉ 1357 Washington Street ☎ 617/423-0555 🚇 Back Bay/South End

Cambridge

This historic and multicultural city across the river from Boston is one of America's greatest academic centers, thanks to universities such as Harvard and the Massachusetts Institute of Technology.

AGASSIZ HALL

UNIVERSITY MUSEUM

HARVARD UNIVERSITY
MUSEUM OF NATURAL HISTORY
ENTRANCE TO ALL EXHIBITS

The facade of the Museum of Natural History (left) and displays (below and right)

CAMBRIDGE

★

TOP 25

Few universities have such an enviable collection. The pieces in Harvard's three art museums, each of which has its own character, are of world-class quality.

Fogg Art Museum Concentration is on Italian early-Renaissance art, with artists such as Simone Martini, Bernardo Daddi and Filippo Lippi.

Busch-Reisinger Museum Expressionist art of Central and Northern Europe features, with Bauhaus objects and work by Kandinsky and Klee.

Arthur M. Sackler Museum One of the world's best Chinese jade collections where Chinese bronzes, Japanese prints, and Greco-Roman antiquities are the highlights.

Renovations During reconstruction of the Fogg, beginning in 2008, full collections will not be shown. Selections from it and the Busch-Reisinger will be shown temporarily at the Sackler.

Harvard Museum of Natural History (HMNH) More than 3,000 models of 830 plant species are all so realistic you cannot believe they are made of glass. Elsewhere are wild animals and birds, plus rocks and minerals, including precious gems.

Peabody Museum One of the world's finest collections recording human culture, especially strong in Native American peoples, is interpreted to provide historical and cultural backgrounds. The museum shop is a treasure trove.

HIGHLIGHTS

- Impressionists (Fogg)
- Jade (Sackler)
- Glass flowers (HMNH)
- Native American exhibits (Peabody)

Harvard Square and Harvard University

HIGHLIGHTS

● Harvard Yard
● Radcliffe Yard
● Browsing in a bookshop all evening

TIPS

● Harvard is one place where a guided tour is essential. Stop in the Holyoke Arcade at 1350 Massa-chusetts Avenue to sign up for a free one.
● Stroll down to the river to watch the crew teams practice.

One of the most significant strands in the fabric of Bostonian life is the academic scene. In Cambridge you can walk through hallowed Harvard Yard in the footsteps of the great, then enjoy the funky scene in Harvard Square.

Harvard University Among the first things the Massachusetts Bay colonists did was to provide for the training of ministers, and thus was founded, in 1636, what became one of the world's most respected seats of learning. Most of its historic buildings are in Harvard Yard, entered across the street from the First Parish Church. Ahead, in front of Bulfinch's granite University Hall, is a statue by Daniel Chester French of benefactor John Harvard.

The elegant 18th-century redbrick halls grouped around this, the Old Yard, are dormitories. Behind

Clockwise from left: A café in Harvard Square; students gather around the ornate gateway into a Harvard college; students on lawns outside Widener Memorial Library; a street-musician entertains in Harvard Square; New Yard in the fall (autumn); pedestrians and students mingle in Harvard Square

University Hall is New Yard, with Memorial Church on the left facing the pillared facade of Widener Library. Pass beside H. H. Richardson's Sever Hall to emerge in Quincy Street opposite the Carpenter Center for the Visual Arts, the only Le Corbusier building in North America. The Fogg Art Museum (▷ 89) is next door. Radcliffe Institute is alongside Cambridge Common, around the lovely Radcliffe Yard.

Harvard Square The newsstand by the T is a famous landmark in this "square," which is actually more of a district than a square. Here you can watch chess, listen to street musicians, sit in an outdoor café, eat dessert at any time of day in Finale (Mt. Auburn Street), shop for trendy clothes, browse in bookshops or go to a club for jazz or reggae.

THE BASICS

www.harvard.edu
🔗 B1/B2
✉ Harvard University: Harvard Yard, Peabody Street, Cambridge
☎ City of Cambridge Visitor Information Booth: 617/497-1630; University: 617/495-1573
🕐 Daily
🍴 Plenty
🚇 Harvard Square
💲 Free
❓ Campus tours Mon–Fri 10, 2, Sat 2

More to See

LONGFELLOW HOUSE AND BRATTLE STREET

In the pre-Revolutionary 1770s the land on either side of Brattle Street was owned by loyalist families, forced to quit when the Patriots took over the area in 1774. Henry Wadsworth Longfellow came to No. 105 Longfellow Street as a lodger in 1837 and wrote many of his poems here. Take the tour through the dining room, parlor, library, bedrooms and, of course, Longfellow's study.

➕ A1/A2 ✉ 105 Brattle Street, Cambridge ☎ 617/876-4492 🕐 Summer Wed–Sun 10–4.30 🚇 Harvard Square, then pleasant walk (0.5 miles/0.8km) 💵 Inexpensive

MIT BUILDINGS

MIT has some impressive modern architecture. You are free to wander around the campus. Seek out Eero Saarinen's serene round chapel (1955). Don't miss Frank Gehry's latest whimsical Ray and Maria Stata Center for Computer, Information and Intelligence Sciences (2004), on Vassar Street. On and near Ames

Street the low Wiesner and the tall Green buildings are the work of I. M. Pei (1964, 1985).

➕ E4 ✉ Massachusetts Avenue, Vassar Street, Ames Street 🚇 Kendall 💵 Free

MIT SCULPTURES

On the campus are two Henry Moore reclining figure pieces (1963, 1976), Alexander Calder's black steel *The Big Sail* (1965) and Michael Heizer's pink granite *Guennette* (1977).

➕ E5 ✉ Memorial Drive 🕐 Daily 🚇 Kendall 💵 Free

MOUNT AUBURN CEMETERY, CAMBRIDGE

A little out of the way, but a beautiful place. It was built in 1831 as the country's first rural garden cemetery and is still very popular with bird and plant lovers. If it's a nice day you could walk from Longfellow House. Longfellow now rests here, as does the artist Winslow Homer.

➕ Off map at A1 ✉ Mount Auburn Street, Cambridge ☎ 617/547-7105 🕐 Daily 🚇 Harvard, then walk or Watertown bus

Mount Auburn Cemetery

Portrait of Henry Wadsworth Longfellow

MORE TO SEE

★

CAMBRIDGE

Harvard Square

Harvard Square, compact with noteworthy institutions, makes an excellent walk. Follow its circumference to see its delights.

DISTANCE: 1 mile (1.6km) **ALLOW:** 3–4 hours

START

JOHN HARVARD STATUE, HARVARD YARD (▷ 90) ✚ B2 🚇 Harvard Square

1 Begin on the Harvard University Green, on the site of the country's oldest college. Walk out of the gates and cross Massachusetts Avenue.

2 Go straight down Church Street, passing numerous shops, until Church hits Brattle Street (▷ 92). Take a right on Brattle.

3 Continue down Brattle Street, passing stately mansions, on the way to the Longfellow House (▷ 92), where Henry Wadsworth Longfellow once lived.

4 Turn around on Brattle and head back toward Harvard Square, passing the American Repertory Theatre (▷ 96) on the way.

END

CAMBRIDGE COMMON (▷ 91) ✚ B2 🚇 Harvard Square

8 Follow Massachusetts Avenue up to Cambridge Common, a magnet for students and professors looking to relax.

7 Stop into The Coop (▷ 94), Harvard's renowned bookstore. Turn right on Massachusetts Avenue about one block, and on the right find Toscanini's—the source for some of Boston's best ice cream.

6 Farther up, pass the Brattle Theatre (▷ 96), an independent cinema and one of the Square's most revered cultural stops. Follow Brattle to the left, where it meets up with Massachusetts Avenue.

5 In the last blocks of Brattle, duck into the row's unique stores and gift shops.

CAMBRIDGE

WALK

Shopping

ABODEON

A stockpile of modern and retro housewares. The vintage furniture is particularly impressive, though you may also want to pick up a few pieces of tableware (from local and global makers) while you're at it.

➕ Off map at B1 ✉ 1731 Massachusetts Avenue
☎ 617/497-0137
🚇 Harvard Square

BEADWORKS

A well-organized little one-room shop filled with small bins of everything you need to make your own jewelry—semi-precious stones, ceramic beads, clasps, wire and more.

➕ B2 ✉ 23 Church Street
☎ 617/868-9777
🚇 Harvard Square

CALLIOPE

A look in the window of this little shop makes you want to be a kid—or have one to buy for. Clothes in creamy colors and soft snuggly fabrics, creative and imaginative toys in sturdy materials, well-chosen children's books and music, and a genial staff make shopping here a pleasure.

➕ B2 ✉ 33 Brattle Street
☎ 617/876-4149 🚇 Harvard

CAMBRIDGE ANTIQUE MARKET

Another large Cambridge cooperative. Dealers sell china, glass, quilts, clothes, silver, jewelry and collectibles.

➕ Off map at G3 ✉ 201 Monsignor O'Brien Highway, diagonally opposite the Lechmere T ☎ 617/868-9655
🕐 Closed Mon 🚇 Lechmere

CAMBRIDGE ARTISTS' COOPERATIVE

Quilts, weaving, jewelry, scarves—all made locally.

➕ B2 ✉ 59a Church Street
☎ 617/868-4434
🚇 Harvard Square

CARDULLO'S

www.cardullos.com
Crammed with international specialty foods, first-rate baked goods and the fixings for gift baskets, this family-run fixture is the place to pick up all your favorite foods and ingredients.

➕ A2 ✉ 6 Brattle Street
☎ 617/491-8888
🚇 Harvard Square

CURIOUS GEORGE GOES TO WORDSWORTH

WordsWorth's children's bookshop, full of delights.

BOOKSTORES

Cambridge, and Harvard Square in particular, has an amazing concentration of independent bookshops; just a handful are mentioned here. Pick up a complete guide from the information kiosk by Harvard Square T. Chainstores such as Borders and Barnes & Noble are to be found throughout Boston and Cambridge.

➕ B2 ✉ 1 JFK Street
☎ 617/498-0062
🚇 Harvard Square

DAKINI

Everything fleece for men, women and children. Fleece boxer shorts, anyone? Designed more for urban style than rugged outdoor wear. You'll find the store between Harvard and Porter squares.

➕ Off map at B1 ✉ 1704 Massachusetts Avenue
☎ 617/864-7661
🚇 Harvard Square, then walk or bus 7

GROLIER POETRY BOOKSHOP

The US's only shop devoted entirely to poetry.

➕ B2 ✉ 6 Plympton Street, Cambridge ☎ 617/547-4648
🚇 Harvard Square

HARVARD BOOKSTORE

Known for academic titles and other nonfiction. New and used books.

➕ B2 ✉ 1256 Massachusetts Avenue, Cambridge
☎ 617/661-1515
🚇 Harvard Square

HARVARD COOP

A peaceful oasis of children's books in the store's basement. A calm, quiet place to browse.

➕ B2 ✉ 1400 Massachusetts Avenue ☎ 617/499-2000
🚇 Harvard Square

HARVARD SQUARE

Cambridge's Harvard Square is a maze of

streets with dozens of bookshops (many stay open all evening), music shops and clothes stores (new and secondhand) much of it geared for students. It's an entertaining place, too, with a wide variety of restaurants and cafés. Check out Brattle Street, Church Street, Eliot Street (with the Charles Square complex just off), JFK Street and Dunster Street. As some of the chains have moved into the area, so some of the smaller local shops have moved, or opened up, just north of Harvard and there's now a clutch of funky clothes and gift shops on Massachusetts Avenue heading toward Porter Square.

HIDDEN SWEETS
There's a lot more than candy inside, although you'll find the traditional "Boston Baked Beans" and maple sweets. Look here for lower prices on Harvard and Red Sox insignia items, and for smart-alec pins, bumper stickers and notepapers that proclaim your progressive politics.
➕ B2 ✉ 25 Brattle Street ☎ 617/497-2600 Ⓣ Harvard

JASMINE SOLA AND SOLA MEN
Chic young designer clothes and shoes in Harvard Square.
➕ A2 ✉ 37 Brattle Street ☎ 617/354-6043 Ⓣ Harvard Square

LEAVITT & PEIRCE INC.
A 118-year-old tobacco shop peddling bins of tobacco, pipes, men's shaving supplies and vintage chess sets.
➕ B2 ✉ 1316 Massachusetts Avenue ☎ 617/547-0576 Ⓣ Harvard Square

MDF
Modern Designer Furnishings: finely crafted picture frames, vases, serving pieces, lamps and small tables.
➕ A2 ✉ 19 Brattle Street ☎ 617/491-2789 Ⓣ Harvard Square

MINT JULEP
Attractive, stylish, but accessible and timeless clothing in luscious fabrics and colors are the style here. Accessories are equally well chosen, and the staff is helpful.
➕ B2 ✉ 8 Church Street ☎ 617/576-6468 Ⓣ Harvard

NOMAD
Baskets handmade in Mexico, Asian masks, carved wooden switch-

plates from Brazil, and jewelry and clothing from Europe—the global market makes its way to the colorful shelves of Nomad.
➕ Off map at B1 ✉ 1741 Massachusetts Avenue ☎ 617/497-6677 Ⓣ Porter Square

STELLABELLA TOYS
This shop repeatedly wins awards for its selection of first-class, imaginative playthings.
➕ C2 ✉ 1360 Cambridge Street ☎ 617/491-6290 Ⓣ Central Square

TESS
Stylish, classic clothes, shoes and accessories for men and women. The cashmere sweater collection and racks of apparel by Italian designers are particularly impressive.
➕ A2 ✉ 20 Brattle Street ☎ 617/846-8377 Ⓣ Harvard Square

URBAN OUTFITTERS
Where the young come to get that rugged look. Funky household goods.
➕ B2 ✉ 11 JFK Street ☎ 617/864-0070 Ⓣ Harvard Square

VIA VAI
Fine women's clothing, from international as well as local designers. Also a small but tasteful selection of accessories.
➕ B2 ✉ 63 JFK Street ☎ 617/497-9959 Ⓣ Harvard Square

OUTLETS

Wrentham Village, Worcester Common and Fall River are three of New England's big factory outlets—where clothes, shoes and household goods are available at discounts of up to 65 percent off the normal retail price—that are within in an hour of central Boston.

CAMBRIDGE

SHOPPING

and Nightlife

AMERICAN REPERTORY THEATRE
www.amrep.org
A highly regarded professional repertory company based in Harvard Square, staging classical and original drama.
➕ A2 ✉ Loeb Drama Center, 64 Brattle Street, Cambridge
☎ 617/547-8300
🚇 Harvard Square

BALLET THEATRE OF BOSTON
Directed by José Mateo, this notable professional company performs a community-friendly mix of classical and contemporary ballet.
➕ B2 ✉ 400 Massachusetts Avenue, Cambridge
☎ 617/354-7467
🚇 Harvard Square

BRATTLE THEATRE
www.brattlefilm.org
Vintage films and film festivals attract connoisseurs to this small, one-screen theater.
➕ A2 ✉ 40 Brattle Street, Cambridge ☎ 617/876-6837
🚇 Harvard Square

CAN-TAB LOUNGE
www.cantab-lounge.com
The dive of choice for R&B, bluegrass and folk performances is also home to 1950s crooner Little Joe Cook, who still performs his hit song "Peanut" here on Friday and Saturday nights.
➕ C3 ✉ 738 Massachusetts Avenue ☎ 617/354-2685
🚇 Central Square

CLUB PASSIM
www.clubpassim.com
The Cambridge area's premier folk music venue attracts both up-and-coming and established performers.
➕ B2 ✉ 47 Palmer Street, Cambridge ☎ 617/492-7679
🚇 Harvard Square

GREEN STREET GRILL
www.greenstreetgrill.com
This restaurant in Cambridge serves spicy Caribbean food, accompanied by live Latin, world beat, salsa and jazz.
➕ D4 ✉ 280 Green Street ☎ 617/876-1655
🕐 Dinner daily from 5.30pm
🚇 Central, then short walk

HARPER'S FERRY
www.harpersferryboston.com
Local, regional and national blues and roots rock performers continue

---

ALTERNATIVE DANCE

Contemporary and ethnic dance troupes perform at venues all over the city and beyond. In Boston, these include the **Dance Collective** (☎ 781/861-0735; www.dancecollective.org). In Cambridge, look for the **Multicultural Arts Center** (✉ 41 2nd Street ☎ 617/577-1400; www.cmacusa.org) and the **Dance Complex** (✉ 536 Massachusetts Avenue ☎ 617/547-9363; www.dancecomplex.org).

to keep this casual place hopping.
➕ B2 ✉ 156 Brighton Avenue ☎ 617/254-7380
🚇 Harvard Square

HARVARD FILM ARCHIVE
http://hcl.harvard.edu/hfa
Daily showings of cult and independent films at Harvard's Carpenter Center for the Visual Arts.
➕ B2 ✉ 24 Quincy Street, Cambridge
☎ 617/495-4700
🚇 Harvard Square

HASTY PUDDING THEATER
www.hastypudding.org
Home to the touring Hasty Pudding Theatricals company and to the American Repertory Theatre's annual "New Stages" series of contemporary plays.
➕ B2 ✉ 12 Holyoke Street, Cambridge
☎ 617/495-5205
🚇 Harvard Square

THE MIDDLE EAST
www.mideastclub.com
The premier venue for alternative rock for not only Cambridge, but also Boston. The Middle Eastern restaurant has three rooms for performers—upstairs, downstairs, and in the restaurant.
➕ C3 ✉ 472/480 Massachusetts Avenue
☎ 617/864-3278
🚇 Central Square

REGATTABAR

www.regattabarjazz.com
First-class jazz acts come to Harvard Square at this classy bar in The Charles Hotel (▷ 112).
🕂 A2 ⊠ 1 Bennett Street, Cambridge
☎ 617/864-1200 or 617/876-7777
🕔 Closed Mon 🚇 Harvard Square

RYLES

www.rylesjazz.com
Another Cambridge hot spot, in Inman Square, with food downstairs. Emphasis is on Latin jazz. Weekly learn-to-salsa

8.30pm, Sun brunch: 10–3
🚇 Central Square then long walk or bus 83; Harvard then bus 69 along Cambridge Street

A BIT OF VARIETY
Fans of old-time vaudeville might like to take a trip out of Boston to Beverly, where Le Grand David and His Own Spectacular Magic Company offer good old-fashioned entertainment at:
Cabot Street Cinema Theater
⊠ 286 Cabot Street
☎ 978/927-3677
🕔 Most Suns

Latin dance night.
🕂 E3 ⊠ 212 Hampshire Street, Cambridge
☎ 617/876-9330
🕔 Music: Tue–Sun from

SANDERS THEATRE

www.fas.harvard.edu
A 1,200-seat neo-Gothic theater at Harvard, with classical and world music. Despite its size the 180-degree stage design allows an imtimate feel.
🕂 B2 ⊠ Quincy Street at Cambridge Street, Cambridge ☎ 617/496-2222
🚇 Harvard Square

Restaurants

PRICES

Prices are approximate, based on a 3-course meal for one person.
$$$	over $40
$$	$20–$40
$	under $20

BOMBAY CLUB ($$)

Buffet lunch is excellent value in this comfortable Indian restaurant, but the view over Harvard Square is captivating anytime.
🕂 B2 ⊠ 57 JFK Street, Harvard Square
☎ 617/661-8100 🕔 Lunch, dinner Mon–Fri; brunch, dinner Sat, Sun
🚇 Harvard Square

BROTHER JIMMY'S ($)

A raucous, fun slice of Southern barbecue culture. Stop in for the messy, spicy ribs, high-octane cocktails and jumpin' atmosphere.
🕂 B2 ⊠ 96 Winthrop Street
☎ 617/547-7427
🚇 Harvard Square

CAFFÈ PARADISO ($)

www.caffeparadiso.com
The perfect place in Harvard Square to grab a slice of torte, a scoop of gelato or panini. The casual sit-down café's wide windows look out to the Square's busy sidewalks.

🕂 B2 ⊠ 1 Eliot Square
☎ 617/868-3240
🚇 Harvard Square

CASABLANCA ($$)

This restaurant is a popular hangout for Harvard folk and young professionals, and serves good appetizers and Mediterranean fare.
🕂 A2 ⊠ 40 Brattle Street
☎ 617/876-0999 🕔 Lunch, dinner Sun–Thu, dinner only Fri–Sat 🚇 Harvard Square

CHEZ HENRI ($–$$)

www.chezhenri.com
Cuban flavors meet classic French dishes in Cambridge's funky, chic bistro. The dining room

serves a full menu of sophisticated dishes on one side, while the bar offers excellent Cuban sandwiches and cocktails on the other.

🔲 A1 ✉ 1 Shephard Street
☎ 617/354-8980
🚇 Harvard Square

CRAIGIE STREET BISTROT ($$$)

www.craigiestreetbistrot.com
The menu is so interesting and tempting that regulars opt for the "Chef's Whim" four- or six-course tasting menus offered Wednesday and Sunday after 9pm. You can be sure that any dish at this exceptionally good bistro uses only the freshest local ingredients.

🔲 A1 ✉ 5 Craigie Circle
☎ 617/497-5511 🚇 Harvard

HI-RISE BREAD COMPANY ($)

Alfresco coffee and good pastries in Harvard Square's Blacksmith House. Built 1811, this was inspiration for Henry Wadsworth Longfellow's poem "Village Black-smith."

🔲 A2 ✉ 56 Brattle Street, Cambridge ☎ 617/492-3003
🚇 Harvard Square

L. A. BURDICK CHOCOLATE ($)

www.burdickchocolate.com
If heaven were a chocolate shop it might look something like this café.

🔲 A2 ✉ 52 Brattle Street, Cambridge ☎ 617/491-4340
🚇 Harvard Square

LEGAL SEA FOODS ($$)

www.legalseafoods.com
Popular seafood chain serving good fish.

🔲 F4 ✉ 5 Cambridge Center, Kendall Square
☎ 617/864-3400 🕐 Hours vary 🚇 Kendall

OM RESTAURANT & LOUNGE ($$–$$$)

Easily Harvard Square's most sophisticated scene. Enjoy an oil-infused martini in the beautiful downstairs lounge (with a wall of water and Tibetan paintings) before heading upstairs for contemporary Asian-inspired cuisine.

🔲 B2 ✉ 57 JFK Street
☎ 617/576-2800
🚇 Harvard Square

RIALTO ($$$)

www.rialto-restaurant.com
Star chef Jody Adams whips up a superb Mediterranean menu made from local ingredients and produce. More casual, but equally delicious, food is served in the restaurant's bar area.

🔲 A2 ✉ The Charles Hotel,

BRUNCH

Henrietta's Table ($$–$$$)
At The Charles Hotel
(▷ 112). Awarded the "Best Brunch in Boston," other meals are equally inventive.

🔲 B2 ✉ 1 Bennett Street, Cambridge ☎ 617/661-5005
🕐 Breakfast, brunch, lunch and dinner daily
🚇 Harvard Square

1 Bennett Street ☎ 617/661-5005 🚇 Harvard Square

SANDRINE'S ($$$)

www.sandrines.com
The serene decor and amiable service set the tone for relaxed dining on Alsatian dishes worthy of full attention. Don't skip the soups or the salads (perhaps Cortland apples, blue cheese and spiced cashews) en route to the silky scallops or a hearty *choucroute garnie* of meats and sausages cooked in Riesling.

🔲 A2 ✉ 8 Holyoke Street
☎ 617/497-5300 🚇 Harvard

UPSTAIRS ON THE SQUARE ($$–$$$)

www.upstairsonthesquare.com
Whimsical in its interior as much as in its cuisine, this elaborately appointed, multifloor restaurant excels at creations like Gruyère tart with Asian pear and black truffle.

🔲 B2 ✉ 91 Winthrop Street
☎ 617/864-1933
🚇 Harvard Square

Z SQUARE ($)

www.Z-square.com
Whether it's a lunch of "ZLT"—a BLT with avocado on sourdough bread—or dinner of cod encrusted in toasted almonds, you can be certain of flavorful creative takes in this classy little dining room. Upstairs, a take-out counter is good for picnics or lunch-on-the-run.

🔲 A2 ✉ 14 JFK Street
☎ 617/576-0101 🚇 Harvard

RESTAURANTS

CAMBRIDGE

You could easily spend weeks in Boston and not come to the end of all the city has to offer. Dozens of historical and cultural attractions lie within easy day-trip reach and are worth exploring in their own right.

Farther Afield

EAST
SOMERVILLE

SOMERVILLE

CAMBRIDGE

CAMBRIDGE STREET

MONSIGNOR

2A

28

3 2

SOLDIERS FIELD ROAD

MASSACHUSETTS AVENUE

EAST
CAMBRIDGE

ALLISTON

90

20

30

MEMORIAL DRIVE

Charles River Basin

COMMONWEALTH AVENUE

JFK National
Historic Site

BEACON STREET

BACK BAY

COOLIDGE
CORNER

LONGWOOD

Back Bay
Fens

HUNTINGTON AVENUE

2

BROOKLINE
VILLAGE

ROXBURY
CROSSING

BROOKLINE
HILL

BOYLSTON STREET

9

Frederick Law Olmsted
National Historic Site

ROXBURY

COLUMBUS AVENUE

MARTIN LUTHER KING BLVD

Olmsted
Park

Jamaica
Pond

Larz
Anderson
Park

Larz Anderson
Auto Museum

Gillette Stadium,
Foxborough

Arnold
Arboretum

WASHINGTON STREET

Franklin
Park Zoo

SEAVER STREET

28

Boston Harbor Islands

TOP 25

Fort Warren on Georges Island

Gather wild raspberries, picnic on a beach, visit a ruined fort—all within sight of the city? These wildernesses are ringed by Boston, its airport and suburbs: It's just incredible they've escaped development.

America's newest national park Once defensive sites and home to prisons and poorhouses, the Boston Harbor Islands were largely ignored until they became a National Recreation Area in 1996. People are beginning to appreciate these havens of wildlife, so near, yet so distant in feel.

Island hopping It's a 45-minute ferry ride from Long Wharf to Georges Island. From here water taxis loop to Lovells, Peddocks, Bumpkin and Grape. The islands are small, so you can visit more than one in a day; each has its own character. Georges attracts most visitors. All have picnic areas (there's no fresh water). Take guided walks, hike trails on your own or just beachcomb (beaches are mostly pebbly). Lovells has a sandy, supervised swimming beach.

Something for everyone On Georges clamber over Fort Warren (find the hidden spiral staircase and get superb views of the city). Peddocks and Lovells also have ruined forts. Bumpkin is where to pick raspberries. Join the hares on Lovells; study the wildlife in the rock pools, salt marsh and woodland on Peddocks; and on Grape, crunch along beaches covered in iridescent blue mussel shells.

JFK Library and Museum

The exterior of the JFK Library and Museum (below and right)

"A man may die, nations may rise and fall, but an idea lives on," said the late president John F. Kennedy, whose life, leadership and legacy are brilliantly evoked in this dramatic museum by the sea.

The setting The presidential library and its museum, constructed in 1979, are housed in an I. M. Pei building on Dorchester Bay, 4 miles (6.5km) southeast of downtown Boston. The building's two towers, of dark glass and smooth white concrete, command fine views of the city, the bay and Boston Harbor Islands. The lawns, dune grass and wild roses on the grounds recall the Kennedy summer home on Cape Cod.

The New Museum An introductory film covers Kennedy's early years, from his childhood to the 1960 presidential campaign. Re-created settings include the White House corridors and the Oval Office, complete with the coconut inscribed "HELP" that led to his rescue after his naval ship sank in the Pacific. Videos cover significant events such as the Cuban Missile Crisis, space exploration and the assassination. Family photographs and exhibits cover the life and work of Jacqueline Kennedy Onassis.

The Presidential Library This is one of 11 presidential libraries holding the papers of 11 of the US presidents since Herbert Hoover. The Presidential Library System allows presidents to establish a library and museum.

THE BASICS

www.jfklibrary.org
✚ Off map at J9
✉ Columbia Point, Dorchester
(Route 3/I-93 exit 15)
☎ 617/514-1600
🕐 Daily 9–5
🍴 Café on premises
🚇 JFK/Uni of Mass., then free shuttle bus
♿ Excellent
💰 Moderate. Boston CityPass applies
❓ Shop

HIGHLIGHTS

● The building, its setting and views
● Introductory video
● Oval Office
● Film and sound clips

TIP

● At the JFK Library, don't miss the Hemingway collection, which includes manuscripts and artifacts from the late, great writer.

More to see

ARNOLD ARBORETUM
Stunning in all seasons, this hilly park is part of the "Emerald Necklace."
➕ Off map at B9 ✉ 125 Arborway, Jamaica Plain ☎ 617/524-1718 🚇 Orange line to Forest Hills 🎫 Free

FRANKLIN PARK ZOO
Wander through an African Tropical Forest, stroke small animals at the Children's Zoo, visit the lions, then picnic in the hills and meadows.
➕ Off map at G9 ✉ 1 Franklin Park Road ☎ 617/541-5466 🕐 Daily 🍴 Café or picnic 🚇 Forest Hills, then bus 16 🎫 Moderate

FREDERICK LAW OLMSTED NATIONAL HISTORIC SITE
The country's most famous landscape architect designed Boston Common, Central Park and the US Capitol grounds. At his workshop, visitors can tour the grounds and arrange week-end walking tours.
➕ Off map at A9 ✉ 99 Warren Street ☎ 617/566-1689 🕐 Reopening 2010 🚇 Brookline Hills (Green line D) then 0.75-mile (1.2km) walk 🎫 Free

GILLETTE STADIUM
Gillette Stadium (an hour's drive south or train from South Station) is home to the New England Patriots (August–September) and the men's pro soccer team, New England Revolution (April through July).
➕ Off map at B9 ✉ Route 1, Foxborough ☎ Ticketmaster: 617/931-2000

JFK NATIONAL HISTORIC SITE
Take a trip to Camelot at President Kennedy's boyhood home, filled with photographs and other memorabilia.
➕ A7 ✉ 83 Beals Street ☎ 617/566-7937 🕐 May–Oct Wed–Sun 10–4.30 🚇 Coolidge Corner (Green line C) 🎫 Tour inexpensive

LARZ ANDERSON AUTO MUSEUM
The world's largest private automobile collection—highlights include antique Mercedes and French cars.
➕ Off map at B9 ✉ 15 Newton Street, Brookline ☎ 617/522-6547 🕐 Tue–Sun, Mon hols and in vacation weeks 10–5 🚇 Cleveland Circle (Green line C), then bus 51 (not Sun) 🎫 Inexpensive

Blazing fall color at the Arnold Arboretum

PLYMOUTH

The Pilgrims left Plymouth, England, for the New World on the *Mayflower*. Their landing of 1620 (the exact location is debated) is commemorated on the waterfront by Plymouth Rock, the town having been named after the Devon port from where they set sail. Don't expect a boulder, however; most visitors are disappointed by the small size of the granite stone.

A more satisfying way to get in touch with the history of Massachusetts' first settlers is to visit them at Plimoth Plantation, a meticulously researched reproduction Pilgrim settlement 3 miles (5km) south. Here interpreters in period costume chat with visitors while getting on with their chores. The excellent curators work hard to make the village site accessible; the most recent exhibits detail how the Pilgrims' diet related to the seasons. At another exhibit, Hobbamock's Homesite, the Native Americans on whose ancestors' land the Pilgrims settled tell of their experiences. Also affiliated with the museum is the *Mayflower II*, a seaworthy replica of the ship that the Pilgrims sailed from England to the New World. Costumed interpreters provide below-decks tours and insight into the perilous crossing.

Plymouth is a popular destination and offers motels, restaurants and other attractions catering to visitors—some of them authentic, others tacky. One worth a stop is the Pilgrim Hall Museum, which is full of impressive artifacts once owned by the Pilgrims, including furniture, clothing and armor. While not quite as authentic, the Plymouth National Wax Museum will delight children, with key events in the history of the colony depicted in dioramas with life-size figures. One of the best times to visit Plymouth is during Thanksgiving, when the town pulls out all the stops with a parade and other events—and modern-day Native Americans stage an annual protest they call the "National Day of Mourning."

THE BASICS

www.visit-plymouth.com
Distance: 50 miles (80km)
Journey Time: 1 hour
☎ Plimoth Plantation: 508/746-1622
🕐 Plimoth Plantation and *Mayflower II*: Apr–Nov
🚉 From South Station
♿ Plimoth Plantation, *Mayflower II*: expensive. Pilgrim Hall Museum: moderate
ℹ Destination Plymouth
✉ 170 Water Street, Suite 10c
☎ 800/872-1620

HIGHLIGHTS

● Plimoth Plantation
● Hobbamock's Homesite
● The *Mayflower II*
● Plymouth Rock
● Pilgrim Hall Museum

FARTHER AFIELD

EXCURSIONS

LEXINGTON AND CONCORD

These lovely towns are immortalized by events that sparked the first shots of the Revolution.

It was to Lexington, where Patriot leaders were staying, that Paul Revere made his famous ride to warn of British plans to seize a cache of arms in Concord. It was on Concord's North Bridge, on April 19, 1775, that the "shot heard round the world" was fired. Concord has a literary past, too, as the home of influential early 19th-century writers and thinkers Henry David Thoreau, Ralph Waldo Emerson, Nathaniel Hawthorne and Louisa May Alcott. Visit their houses, and their graves in Sleepy Hollow Cemetery.

SALEM

To many, Salem means witches, so it's not surprising to find a range of interpretations of the mass hysteria that hit the town in the 1690s.

The most popular attraction is the Salem Witch Museum, which treads a fine line between cheap thrills and historical accuracy in telling the macabre tale of the trials that claimed 19 lives. Other sites worth visiting are the Witch House, which belonged to the presiding judge, and the affecting memorial to the victims on Salem Common.

Less well known but far more striking once you're there is that the town also has a rich maritime history and some of the best Federal architecture in America. In the 18th and early 19th centuries Salem's prosperous shipbuilders, merchants and sea captains built graceful houses and filled them with beautiful things. Many of these objects are in the Peabody Essex Museum.

From left: Captain Parker statue in Lexington; band-stand; Roger Conant statue; House of the Seven Gables in Salem; Witch Museum sign

The places to rest your head around Boston run from family-run bed-and-breakfasts to elaborate, world-class hotels. The majority are a convenient walking distance from the major sights.

Where to Stay

Introduction

Boston has no shortage of places to stay, all to suit your personal preferences for style, noise level, amenities and location.

Bed-and-Breakfasts and Inns

Bed-and-breakfasts are often run out of a private home. They normally include a modest bedroom, plus a home-cooked breakfast, at a reasonable price. Boston and Cambridge have a number of such establishments in the city. A bit more luxurious and larger than a bed-and-breakfast, the best inns around Boston are often housed in historic buildings or town houses. They also often include breakfast, though sometimes charge a separate fee. Some have such modern amenities as flat-screen televisions, CD players and whirlpool tubs.

Boutique and Luxury Hotels

Over the last several years, a stable of chic, modern small hotels has cropped up. The majority offer stylish, contemporary design, hip restaurants on the property and concierge services. They are mostly in and around downtown Boston. Scattered throughout Boston's most popular neighborhoods (from Back Bay and Downtown to Harvard Square), the area's luxury hotels cater to the traveler's every need and whim. Some offer quirky amenities (books delivered to your room at Harvard Square's Charles Hotel) alongside services such as in-room massages and personal shoppers.

HISTORIC HOTELS

A handful of the city's most history-laden sites are also places you can stay the night. The **Omni Parker House** (▷ 111) is America's longest continuously operating luxury hotel. Opened in 1855, it was the meeting site of a literary group that included Ralph Waldo Emerson and Nathaniel Hawthorne. Later, its dining room gained a place in Boston history as the site of President (then Senator) John F. Kennedy's proposal to Jacqueline Bouvier. The **Fairmont Copley Plaza** (▷ 112) has witnessed many of Boston's grandest celebrations.

Budget Hotels

PRICES

Expect to pay between $75 and $150 per night for a budget hotel.

BEST WESTERN
www.bestwestern.com
Near Fenway Park. 155 rooms; 8 special rooms for visitors with disabilites.
➕ D9 ✉ 342 Longwood Avenue ☎ 617/731-4700 or 800/468-2378; fax 617/731-6273 🚇 Green line D to Longwood

BOSTON INTERNATIONAL YOUTH HOSTEL
www.bostonhostel.org
Dormitories, cooking facilities available. 205 beds.
➕ E8 ✉ 12 Hemenway Street, Back Bay ☎ 617/536-9455; fax 617/424-6558 🚇 Hynes Convention Center

OUT OF TOWN

To reduce hotel costs, consider staying in Concord, Salem or Rockport, all 40–60 minutes from Boston and served by regular train services. Contact:
Concord Chamber of Commerce
☎ 978/369-3120; www.concordmachamberofcommerce.org
Destination Salem
✉ 978/744-3663; www.salem.org
Rockport Chamber of Commerce ✉ 978/546-6575; www.rockportusa.com

CHANDLER INN
www.chandlerinn.com
Basic 56-room hotel in the attractive South End. Gay-friendly. Short walk to Tremont Street restaurant row and Copley Square.
➕ H7 ✉ 26 Chandler Street ☎ 617/482-3450 or 800/842-3450; fax 617/542-3428 🚇 Back Bay/South End

COLLEGE CLUB
www.thecollegeclubofboston.com
You don't have to be a student to book one of the attractive single rooms here. Shared bathrooms.
➕ G6 ✉ 44 Commonwealth Avenue ☎ 617/536-9510

COMFORT INN
www.choicehotels.com
Inexpensive option 3 miles (5km) south of town. Outdoor pool, bowling alley nearby. 133 rooms.
➕ Off map at K9 ✉ 900 Morrissey Boulevard, Dorchester ☎ 617/287-9200 or 800/446-4656; fax 617/282-2365 🚇 JFK/University of Massachusetts, then half-hourly hotel shuttle bus 7am–10pm

THE COPLEY INN
www.copleyinn.com
The classic brick row house has 20 double rooms, each with kitchenette and bath. There's no front desk and no elevator, but the homey atmosphere and central location make it popular.
➕ F7 ✉ 19 Garrison Street

☎ 617-236-0300
🚇 Prudential

JOHN JEFFRIES HOUSE
www.johnjeffrieshouse.com
Four-floor brick inn on Beacon Hill; 46 tiny rooms. The two-room suites are better value.
➕ H5 ✉ 14 David Mugar Way (formerly Embankment Road) at Charles Circle ☎ 617/367-1866; fax 617/742-0313 🚇 Charles/MGH

NEWBURY GUEST HOUSE
www.hagopianhotels.com
Victorian-style rooms—32 in all—in three connected redbrick row houses. Excellent value, popular; reserve well ahead.
➕ G6 ✉ 261 Newbury Street, Back Bay ☎ 617/437-7666 or 800/437-7668; fax 617/6706100 🚇 Copley, Hynes Convention Center

BED-AND-BREAKFAST

Double occupancy in bed-and-breakfast accommodation ranges from $90 to $180.
Try the **Bed-and-Breakfast Agency of Boston**
A helpful, friendly agency that will find you accommodation in historic houses and restored waterfront lofts. Nightly, weekly, monthly and winter rates
(✉ 47 Commercial Wharf ☎ 617/720-3540, 800/248-9262 or 0800 89 5128 from the UK; fax 617/523-576; www.boston-bnbagency.com).

Mid-Range Hotels

BACK BAY HILTON
www.hilton.com
Convenient to the Pru and Hynes centers. 385 rooms.
➕ F7 ✉ 40 Dalton Street, Back Bay ☎ 617/236-1100 or 800/874-0663; fax 617/867-6104 🚇 Prudential, Hynes Convention Center

BEACON HILL HOTEL AND BISTRO
www.beaconhillhotel.com
Thirteen tasteful, unfussy rooms in two linked townhouses. Lovely roof deck.
➕ H5 ✉ 25 Charles Street ☎ 617/723-7575 or 888/959-2442; fax 617/723-7525 🚇 Charles/MGH

BOSTON PARK PLAZA
www.bostonparkplaza.com
Elegant hotel built in 1927, with 950 rooms. Near the Public Garden and Theater District. Family friendly.
➕ H6 ✉ 64 Arlington Street ☎ 617/426-2000 or 800/225-2008; fax 617/423-1708 🚇 Arlington

COLONNADE
www.colonnadehotel.com
Behind the bland 1960s facade of this 285-room hotel near the Pru are traditionally decorated rooms. Rooftop pool. Home of Brasserie Jo.
➕ F7 ✉ 120 Huntington Avenue, Back Bay ☎ 617/ 424-7000 or 800/962-3030; fax 617/424-1717 🚇 Prudential

CONSTITUTION INN
www.constitution.com
Within sight of its namesake ship, this Spartan, nautically themed inn offers military discounts.
➕ K2 ✉ 150 2nd Avenue, Charlestown ☎ 617/241-8400 🚇 North Station

COURTYARD BOSTON TREMONT HOTEL
www.marriott.com
In the heart of the theater district, this branch of the Marriott Courtyard chain inhabits an historic 1925 building.
➕ J6 ✉ 275 Tremont Street ☎ 617/426-1400 🚇 Boylston

ELIOT
www.eliothotel.com
Elegance, comfort and value. 95 rooms and suites with living room and kitchenette.
➕ E6 ✉ 370 Commonwealth Avenue, Back Bay ☎ 617/267-1607 or 800/44 ELIOT; fax 617/536-9114 🚇 Hynes Convention Center

GRYPHON HOUSE
www.gryphonhouseboston.com
Each of the eight rooms at this well-appointed B&B has its own distinct identity. Around the corner from Fenway Park.
➕ E6 ✉ 9 Bay State Road ☎ 617/375-903 🚇 Kenmore

HAMPTON INN & SUITES BOSTON CROSSTOWN CENTER
www.bostonhamptoninn.com
Good value at this modern-feeling hotel on the edge of the South End. Free shuttle to many city attractions.
➕ F7 ✉ 811 Massachusetts Avenue ☎ 617/445-6400 🚇 Massachusetts Avenue (Orange line)

HARBORSIDE INN
www.harborsideinnboston.com
A can't-beat downtown location and elegant furnishings make this independent hotel good value for the money.
➕ K5 ✉ 85 State Street ☎ 617/723-7500 🚇 State

HOTEL MARLOWE

www.hotelmarlowe.com
Overlooking the Charles River near the Science Museum, this elegant hotel is big and boutique at the same time. Rooms are lushly decorated and service is far beyond the price range.
🕂 H3 ⊠ 24 Edwin Land Boulevard ☎ 617/868-8000 or 800/825-7040 🚇 Lechmere

HYATT REGENCY BOSTON

www.regencyboston.hyatt.com
Opened in late 2004, this 22-floor, 500-room hotel is close to Faneuil Hall and the Theater District.
🕂 J6 ⊠ One Avenue de Lafayette ☎ 617/912-1234 or 800/633-7313; fax 617/451-2198
🚇 Downtown Crossing

INN AT HARVARD

www.theinnatharvard.com
Luxurious accommodations characterize this plush hotel affiliated with Harvard University.
🕂 B2 ⊠ 1201 Massachusetts Avenue, Cambridge
☎ 617/491-2222
🚇 Harvard Square

JEWEL OF NEWBURY

www.jewelboston.com
Take an exotic vacation-within-a-vacation with the eye-popping array of antiques from around the world at this intimate Back Bay B&B.
🕂 F7 ⊠ 254 Newbury Street
☎ 617/536-5523
🚇 Hynes Convention Center

KENDALL HOTEL

www.kendallhotel.com
A former firehouse close to MIT and just over the bridge to Boston has been converted into a comfortable boutique hotel, complete with Americana furnishings.
🕂 F4 ⊠ 350 Main Street, Cambridge
☎ 866/566-1300
🚇 Kendall/MIT

LA CAPELLA SUITES

www.lacapellasuites.com
Bare-bones B&B accommodations in the North End give you enviable access to the restaurants and cafés of Hanover Street.
🕂 K4 ⊠ 290 North Street
☎ 617/523-9020
🚇 Haymarket

SOUTH END B&BS

Herbst Haus
www.herbsthaus.com
A Victorian town house in the South End with two comfortable suites.
⊠ Appleton Street
☎ 617/266-0235
🚇 Back Bay/South End

30 Claremont Park
www.30claremontpark.com
Unlike traditional B&Bs, the decor here is smart and modern. A roof deck offers great views.
⊠ 30 Claremont Park
☎ 617/266-7035
🚇 Back Bay/South End

MARY PRENTISS INN

www.maryprentissinn.com
A 20-room, antiques-filled bed-and-breakfast with modern amenities.
🕂 E9 ⊠ 6 Prentiss Street ☎ 617/661-2929; fax 617/661-5989
🚇 Porter Square

OMNI PARKER HOUSE

www.omnihotels.com
A rather staid 551-room, 19th-century hotel, near Boston Common. The Parker House roll and Boston cream pie were invented here.
🕂 J5 ⊠ 60 School Street, Downtown
☎ 617/227-8600 or 800/843-6664; fax 617/742-5729 🚇 Park Street

RADISSON HOTEL

www.radisson.com/bostonma
The Radisson has a convenient Theater District location plus a fitness club, pool, and rooftop sundeck overlooking the city.
🕂 J6 ⊠ 200 Stuart Street
☎ 617/482-1800 🚇 Boylston

SHERATON BOSTON

www.starwood.com/sheraton
1,215 rooms in two 29-floor towers, connected by interior walkways to the Pru and Hynes. Caters to business travelers, but is also family-friendly.
🕂 G7 ⊠ Prudential Center, 39 Dalton Street ☎ 617/236-2000 or 800/325-3535; fax 617/236-1702 🚇 Prudential, Hynes Convention Center

Luxury Hotels

BOSTON HARBOR

www.bhh.com
Modern, elegant, 230-room hotel on the waterfront. It's worth paying a little more for harbor views. Good restaurant, with views.

➕ L5 ✉ 70 Rowes Wharf ☎ 617/439-7000 or 800/752-7077; fax 617/330-945 🚇 Aquarium

THE CHARLES HOTEL

www.charleshotel.com
Modern 293-room hotel in Harvard Square. Home to Henrietta's Table (panel ▷ 98) and Regattabar (▷ 96) jazz club.

➕ B2 ✉ 1 Bennett Street, Cambridge ☎ 617/864-1200 or 800/882-1818; fax 617/864-5715 🚇 Harvard Square

COPLEY SQUARE

www.copleysquarehotel.com
143-room hotel with European flavor. No fitness facility or pool.

➕ G6 ✉ 47 Huntington Avenue, Back Bay ☎ 617/536-9000 or 800/225-7062; fax 617/267-3547 🚇 Copley

FAIRMONT COPLEY PLAZA

www.fairmont.com
A "grand dame" of Boston, with sumptuous decor. 383 rooms.

➕ G6 ✉ 138 St. James Avenue, Back Bay ☎ 617/267-5300 or 800/527-4727; fax 617/267-7668 🚇 Copley

FOUR SEASONS

www.fourseasons.com/boston
Top-notch elegance and service. Aujourd'hui (▷ 61) and Bristol restaurants. 272 rooms.

➕ H6 ✉ 200 Boylston Street, Back Bay ☎ 617/338-4400 or 800/332–3442; fax 617/423-0154 🚇 Arlington

LANGHAM HOTEL

www.langhamhotels.com
Historic 1920s building with luxurious comforts. 326 rooms. Café Fleuri restaurant (▷ 61).

➕ K5 ✉ 250 Franklin Street ☎ 617/451-1900; fax 617/423-2844 🚇 State, Downtown Crossing

LENOX

www.lenoxhotel.com
Built in 1900, this 212-room independent is one of the best.

➕ G6 ✉ 710 Boylston Street ☎ 617/536-5300 or 800/225-7676; fax 617/267-1237 🚇 Copley

THE LIBERTY HOTEL

www.libertyhotel.com
Brilliant transformation of a grim old city jail into a stunning contemporary

hotel with river views. There's just enough tongue-in-cheek reference to its past to be fun.

➕ H4 ✉ 215 Charles Street ☎ 617/224-4000, 866/507-5245 🚇 Charles

MILLENNIUM BOSTONIAN

www.millennium-hotels.com
This 201-room hotel is more intimate than some, and offers comfort without glitz. Seasons Restaurant.

➕ K5 ✉ Faneuil Hall Marketplace ☎ 617/523-3600 or 866/866-8086; fax 617/523–2454 🚇 State, Government Center

NINE ZERO

www.ninezero.com
When the stars are in town, they stay at this chic boutique hotel on the Freedom Trail. Rooms are tricked out with all the latest gadgets and amenities.

➕ J6 ✉ 90 Tremont Street ☎ 617/772-5800 🚇 Park Street

SEAPORT HOTEL

www.seaportboston.com
In Boston's newest downtown neighborhood, the hotel is opposite the World Trade Center and the new Institute of Contemporary Art. It's a class act, with fine dining at Aura, a full spa, in-room wireless and interactive web portal.

➕ M6 ✉ 1 Seaport Lane (Northern Avenue) ☎ 617/385-4000 or 877/732-7678 🚇 World Trade Center

Need to Know

This section contains practical information about getting to Boston and traveling around once you are there, as well as tips, useful phone numbers, money matters and public holidays.

Planning Ahead

When to Go

Summer and fall are peak visiting seasons. Hotels are busy at graduation time (May, June) and rates go up. In October you will get a glimpse of New England's fall foliage (better still farther north). The time between Thanksgiving and New Year are full of seasonal festivities.

TIME

Boston is on Eastern Standard Time, five hours behind GMT, three hours ahead of Los Angeles.

AVERAGE DAILY MAXIMUM TEMPERATURES

JAN	FEB	MAR	APR	MAY	JUN	JUL	AUG	SEP	OCT	NOV	DEC
37°F	37°F	46°F	56°F	66°F	76°F	82°F	80°F	75°F	63°F	52°F	37°F
3°C	3°C	8°C	13°C	19°C	24°C	28°C	26°C	24°C	17°C	11°C	3°C

Spring (April through May) is unpredictable, but can be wonderful, with cool nights and fresh days. This is when you can catch the magnolia blossoms in the Back Bay.

Summer (June through August) is normally pleasantly warm, but occasional heatwaves can see temperatures soaring into the 90s.

Fall (September through November) is warm in September, and crisp in October and November, when the foliage is at its most colorful.

Winter (December through March) is very cold. Even when the sky is blue winds can be biting. Snows occasionally transform the city; a slushy, gray mess inevitably follows.

WHAT'S ON

January *Martin Luther King weekend.*

February *Chinese New Year* (Jan/Feb).

March *Spring Flower Show. St. Patrick's Day Parade.*

April *Patriots' Day* (3rd Mon): Revere's Ride is re-created.

Boston Marathon (3rd Mon). *Kite Festival* (or May): held in Franklin Park.

May *May Fair* in Harvard Square.

Boston Pops Concerts.

June *Battle of Bunker Hill*: reenactment (Sun before Bunker Hill Day, Jun 17).

Boston Globe Jazz Festival.

July *Boston Pops Concerts. Independence celebrations* (week of Jul 4): Boston Pops concert with fireworks, Boston Harborfest music festival and USS *Constitution* turnaround.

Italian feste (festivals, Jul/Aug weekends): North End.

August *Moon Festival*: Colorful processions in Chinatown.

September *Cambridge River Festival*: Events on the river.

Boston Arts Festival: Columbus Waterfront.

October *Columbus Day Parade.*

Head of the Charles Regatta (3rd week).

Boston Symphony Orchestra: Season Oct–Apr.

November *Christmas tree lighting ceremonies*: Faneuil Hall Marketplace and Charles Square, Cambridge.

Boston Ballet–The Nutcracker (Nov–Dec): Wang Center.

December *Tree lighting ceremonies*: Prudential Center, Harvard Square.

Boston Tea Party (mid-Dec): Re-enactment.

Carol concert: Trinity Church.

Boston Online

www.boston.com
The Boston Globe's website has the daily newspaper, with local news, listings and restaurant reviews.

www.boston.citysearch.com
A guide to local events, theater productions, movies, concerts, sports, stores and restaurants. The site tends to feature big-name destinations and happenings, so you'll find everything from top-10 restaurant lists and heavy-hitter museum exhibits to addresses, phone numbers, schedules and maps.

www.bostonphoenix.com
The *Boston Phoenix* is a weekly alternative newspaper that offers detailed arts and entertainment listings, plus restaurant reviews.

www.bostonusa.com
Run by the Greater Boston Convention and Visitors Bureau, this site includes details about attractions, events, hotels and the subway, as well as other useful visitor information.

www.cambridge-usa.org
This is the Cambridge Office for Tourism's site and it contains listings of hotels, restaurants, attractions and arts and entertainment venues, as well as an events calendar and general visitor information for the City of Cambridge.

www.dailycandy.com
Click onto the Boston edition of this national site to find listings for the city's brand new restaurants and hottest stores, eclectic shows and services and other undiscovered gems.

www.mbta.com
The website of the MBTA (Massachusetts Bay Transportation Authority) is the place to look for timetables, maps and fare information for the T (subway), as well as buses and commuter rail services.

PRIME TRAVEL SITES

www.fodors.com
A complete travel-planning site. You can research prices and weather; book air tickets, cars and rooms; ask questions (and get answers) from fellow travelers; and find links to other sites.

www.massvacation.com
Visitor information from the Massachusetts Office of Travel and Tourism. The site includes an accommodation booking service.

www.orbitz.com
An air-fare search engine owned by five US airlines. It frequently offers low-fare specials.

www.discovernewengland .org
This is the official site for the states of New England, if you are planning a visit beyond Boston.

INTERNET CAFÉ

Kinko's
Copy and printing shops that offer internet access.
Locations include:
➕ F5 ✉ 187 Dartmouth Street (Back Bay) ☎ 617/ 262-6188 🕐 24 hours 🚇 Back Bay, Copley 💵 $12 per hour
➕ C2 ✉ Mifflin Place (off Mt. Auburn Street, Harvard Square) ☎ 617/497-0125 🕐 24 hours 🚇 Harvard 💵 $12 per hour

Getting There

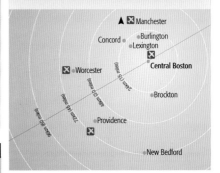

ARRIVING AT LOGAN

Logan Airport is a medium-size, relatively manageable international airport. When you exit from baggage claim, you will be on the lowest level; taxis are readily available outside, as are rental cars—though you will need to take one of the frequently arriving (and complimentary) shuttle buses from your terminal to the car rental company.

CAR RENTAL

Logan Airport has eight car rental companies operating within it; reserve in advance.

Alamo
www.goalamo.com
☎ 800/327-9633

Avis
www.avis.com
☎ 800/831-2847

Budget
www.budgetrentacar.com
☎ 800/527-0700

Dollar
www.dollar.com
☎ 800/800-4000

Enterprise
www.enterprise.com
☎ 800/325-8007

Hertz
www.hertz.com
☎ 800/654-3131

National
www.nationalcar.com
☎ 800/227-7368

Thrifty
www.thrifty.com
☎ 800/367-2277

AIRPORTS

Logan Airport is on an island in Boston Harbor. It has five terminals, hotels and restaurants. Domestic flights also use T. F. Green Airport (Rhode Island), Manchester Airport (New Hampshire) and Worcester Airport (Massachusetts).

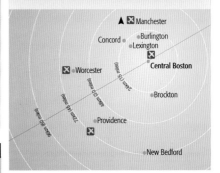

FROM LOGAN AIRPORT

For general airport information ☎ 800/235-6426. "Massport Shuttle" buses run every 20 minutes (5.30am–1am; free) from every terminal to Airport subway (T) station; from here it's a few minutes' journey to central Boston ($2).

Taxis cost $20–$30 (including a tunnel toll, but not tip). Thanks to the new Massachusetts Turnpike extensions from Logan, travel time to and from the airport has been reduced dramatically. Allow roughly 15 minutes to or from Back Bay (▷ panel opposite).

Harbor Express (☎ 617/222-6999) is an exciting way to arrive in central Boston. It's a 10-minute boat ride between Logan and Rowes Wharf in the Financial District, where you can pick up a taxi. Harbor Express also operates between Logan and Quincy and Hull, on the south shore (Mon–Fri 5.55am–11pm, Sat 8am–10pm, Sun 8am–9pm; $10 to Long Wharf). From April through November an on-call City Water Taxi (☎ 617/422-0392) runs from Logan to 20 different waterfront locations (7am–10pm; $10). Shuttle buses connect all terminals with the water taxis.

OTHER AIRPORTS
Domestic flights also use T. F. Green Airport, Rhode Island (☎ 401/737-8222); Manchester Airport, New Hampshire (☎ 603/624-6539); and Worcester Airport, Massachusetts (☎ 508/799-1741). It's then an hour's bus ride to Boston.

ARRIVING BY BUS
Greyhound (☎ 800/231-2222) and Peter Pan Trailways (☎ 800/343-9999) travel between New York and Boston's South Station, and (less frequently) to the rest of the USA and Canada.

ARRIVING BY CAR
From the west: Route I-90, the Massachusetts Turnpike, runs into Boston with exits leading to Cambridge, Storrow Drive (for Fenway, Kenmore Square and Boston Common), the Back Bay, Downtown and I-93 (the Expressway). From the south: 1-93 has one exit for the Massachusetts Turnpike, the Ted Williams Tunnel and Chinatown/South Station. The next exit is to Government Center. From the north: 1-93 has exits for Storrow Drive, for Government Center and the Callahan Tunnel; Purchase Street (for Downtown) and South Station. However drving in Boston is best avoided, due to a lack of parking and narrow streets.

ARRIVING BY TRAIN
Amtrak (☎ 800/872-7245; www.amtrak.com) runs a frequent service between Boston's South Station and Providence, New York, Philadelphia and Washington, D.C. The high-speed Acela service between New York and Boston takes one and a half hours. South Station also serves Washington D.C. and Chicago. Amtrak's Down-easter travels up the coast to Maine from North Station. Trains running in New England tend to arrive and depart on time, but those traveling longer distances are frequently delayed—particularly in winter, when snow slows them down--usually anywhere from 10 minutes to an hour.

TIME TO LOGAN
From downtown Boston, driving to Logan averages 15 minutes. However, during heavy traffic hours (generally 7.30am–9.30am and 4.30pm –6pm on weekdays), count on the ride taking 30 minutes, possibly even 40 in the dead of rush hour. Security lines on international flights can also be quite long, so plan accordingly.

EATING ON THE RUN
At Logan Airport, find:
Legal Sea Foods (where you can also buy live lobsters to package up and take home with you).
Wolfgang Puck, quick and healthy pizzas.
Jasper White's Summer Shack, for fresh New England seafood in a casual atmosphere.
Sam Adams Boston Brewhouse, for pub fare.
Fresh City, wrap sandwiches to go.
Java Coast, for fresh-ground coffee, lattes, bakery goods and sandwiches.

In South Station, find:
Rosie's Bakery, for rich fudges, cakes and brownies.
Au Bon Pain, sandwiches, soups and salads.
Pizzeria Regina, locally loved, small Italian chain.
Surf City Squeeze, for fresh-made fruit smoothies.

Getting Around

BICYCLES

Boston isn't known for being a bicycle-friendly town. If, however, you are looking to get some exercise outside the city, Boston has several bicycle paths that offer pleasant riding. One is the Southwest Corridor, which runs from behind the Massachusetts Avenue T stop all the way out to the Arnold Arboretum in Jamaica Plain. A longer ride is the Minuteman Bikeway, which runs from Davis Square in Somerville all the way out to Bedford—passing by the historical sites in Lexington (▷ 106) on the way.

VISITORS WITH DISABILITIES

An Airport Handicap Van offers a free service between all Logan Airport locations. Use the free "Van Phone" in the baggage-claim area. Public buildings, parking areas and subway stations provide wheelchair access, and many hotels have specially designed rooms. Modern or newly renovated hotels and restaurants tend to be better equipped. For further information contact: New England INDEX ✉ 200 Trapelo Road, Waltham, MA 02452 ☎ 781/642-0248

VISITOR PASSES

● An MBTA (Massachusetts Bay Transportation Authority) Visitor Pass gives unlimited travel for one or seven days ($9.50, $16.50) on all subways, buses and ferries. It is available at vending machines in T stations and online in advance at www.mbta.com. They are NOT available at visitor information centers.

BOATS

● MBTA ferry/Boston Harbor cruises (☎ 617/227-4321) link Long Wharf and Charlestown, Long Wharf and Provincetown.

BUSES

● Buses travel farther out into the suburbs than the T, but the T is much quicker and easier in the center.
● Passengers must have the exact change ($1.50) or Charlie Card.
● For travel farther afield, bus companies operate out of South Station serving destinations throughout New England.

SUBWAY (T)

● Boston's system of subway and elevated trains is known as the T. The five lines—Red, Green, Orange, Silver and Blue—meet in central Boston. "Inbound" and "Outbound" refer to direction in relation to Park Street Station.
● The T is clean and efficient.
● Trains run from 5am (later on Sunday) to 12.45am.
● Rides are now by Charlie Cards, reloadable cards bought at vending machines in stations. Individual rides are $1.85 or $2, depending on the plan selected. These machines are not especially easy for the first-time user, so it is a good idea to visit www.mbta.com in advance, for a clear explanation of the options and operation of machines.
● Free maps are available at the Park Street Station information booth. Note that some maps do not show all stops on the Green line branches.

TAXIS

● Hail taxis on the street or find them at hotels and taxi stands.
● 24-hour taxi services include:
Checker Cab Co ☎ 617/536-7000
Metrocab Cab ☎ 617/242-8000
Town Taxis ☎ 617/536-5000

TRAINS

● MBTA commuter trains leave from North Station for destinations west and north, including Lowell, Concord, Salem, Manchester, Gloucester, Rockport and Ipswich. South Station serves Plymouth and Providence.

DRIVING AND CAR RENTAL
Car rental

● Rental drivers must be at least 21; many companies put the minimum age at 25 or charge extra for those between 21 and 25.
● For car rental companies ▷ 116.
● Consider using the subway to pick up your car from a rental agency on the outskirts of Boston to avoid having to drive in the city.

Driving

● Driving and parking in Boston is challenging.
● Park only in legal spots, or you will be towed. Park in the direction of the traffic.
● Speed limits on the major highways range from 55 to 65mph (90 to 104kph); elsewhere they range from 30 to 45mph (48 to 72kph).
● All front seat passengers must wear a seat belt. Children under 12 years old must sit in the back and use an approved car seat or safety belt.
● You may turn right at a red traffic light if the road ahead is clear, unless signage prohibits it.
● Drink/driving laws are strict. Never drive after drinking; don't keep opened alcohol in the car.
● Look out for one-way streets, especially in downtown Boston where they are legion. Boston taxi drivers are aggressive—the best defense is to yield whenever necessary. And don't be afraid to use your horn!

PEDICABS

A fun and efficient alternative to taxis and subways are the "cycle rickshaws" run by Boston Pedicabs (617/266-2005; www.bostonpedicab.com). The bicycle cabs are easy to find Downtown and can take you to where you are going quickly.

TAXI FARES

At the time of publication, taxi rates are $1.75 for the first 0.8 miles (0.25km), and $0.30 for each additional 0.8 miles (0.25km); or $24 for each hour spent waiting. (Be sure to check rates at the airport.) Trips to and from the airport are subject to additional tolls of $2.25 and $6, respectively; there is no charge for luggage. For trips beyond 12 miles (20km) from downtown Boston, a flat-rate of $2.60 per mile applies.

Essential Facts

TRAVEL INSURANCE

It is vital to have cover for medical expenses, as well as for theft, baggage loss, trip cancellation and accidents. Check your insurance coverage and buy a supplementary policy as needed.

MONEY

The currency is the dollar (=100 cents). Notes (bills) are in denominations of $1, $5, $10, $20, $50 and $100; coins are 25¢ (a quarter), 10¢ (a dime), 5¢ (a nickel) and 1¢ (a penny). You may find that small businesses will not break a $100, $50 or even $20 bill.

5 dollars

10 dollars

50 dollars

100 dollars

ALCOHOL

● It is illegal to drink alcohol in public places such as the T. Do not keep opened bottles of alcohol in the car.
● It is illegal to sell alcohol to anyone under the age of 21. Alcohol is not sold in shops on Sunday or after 11pm Monday through Saturday.

MAGAZINES AND NEWSPAPERS

● Free tourist magazines are found in hotel lobbies, and include discount coupons.
● Listings can be found in the *Boston Globe* (Thursday), the *Boston Herald* (Friday) and the *Boston Phoenix* (Thursday; free).
● *Boston Magazine* (monthly) reviews the Boston scene and gives awards to restaurants.

MAIL

● Letter boxes are gray/blue and have swing-top lids.

MONEY MATTERS

● Nearly all banks have Automatic Teller Machines. Cards registered in other countries that are linked to the Cirrus or Plus networks are accepted. Before leaving, check which network your cards are linked to and ensure your PIN is valid in the US, where four-figure numbers are the norm.
● Credit cards are widely accepted.
● US dollar traveler's checks function like cash in larger hotels and stores.
● Money and traveler's checks can be exchanged at most banks (check fees as they can be high) and many travel centers in central Boston.
● Some businesses may ask for photo identification before cashing traveler's checks.

OPENING HOURS

● Banks: Mon–Fri 9–4, Thu 9–5 or later, Sat 9–2.
● Shops: Mon–Sat 10–6 or later. Closed Sun mornings.

● Museums and sights: Unless otherwise stated, all sights mentioned in this book close on Thanksgiving and Christmas.
● Businesses: Mon–Fri 8 or 9–5.

PUBLIC HOLIDAYS
● **Jan 1** (New Year's Day)
● **3rd Mon in Jan** (Martin Luther King Day)
● **3rd Mon in Feb** (President's Day)
● **Last Mon in May** (Memorial Day)
● **July 4** (Independence Day)
● **1st Mon in Sep** (Labor Day)
● **2nd Mon in Oct** (Columbus Day)
● **Nov 11** (Veterans Day)
● **4th Thu in Nov** (Thanksgiving)
● **Dec 25** (Christmas Day)
● Boston also celebrates: **Mar 17** (Evacuation Day); **3rd Mon in Apr** (Patriots' Day); **Jun 17** (Bunker Hill Day).

SENSIBLE PRECAUTIONS
● Boston is basically a safe city, but it is wise to stick to well-lit and well-populated areas after dark. Avoid the lower half of Washington Street and Boston Common at night.
● Discuss your itinerary with your hotel's reception staff so they can point out any potential problems.
● Be aware of the people around you, especially at night or in quiet areas.
● Keep your wallet or purse out of sight and don't carry valuables or cash openly. Do not carry easily snatched bags and cameras, or put your wallet into your back pocket.
● Keep valuables in your hotel's safe and never carry more money than you need.
● Lost traveler's checks are relatively quick and easy to replace. Keep the numbers of the checks separate from the checks themselves.
● Report any stolen item to the nearest police station, if only to be able to claim on your insurance. The police will fill out the forms your insurance company will need.
● Always lock car doors and keep valuables out of sight.

SMOKING
● Smoking is banned in restaurants unless there is a separate seating area. It is banned in many public places, including the T. Some hotels have no-smoking floors.
● Cambridge is by law smoke-free.

ENTRY REQUIREMENTS
Visitors to the US must show a full passport, valid for at least six months. Most UK citizens and visitors from other countries belonging to the Visa Waiver Program can enter without a visa, but you must have a return or onward ticket. Since US policy changes frequently, be sure to check with the US Embassy, London (☎ 020 7499 9000; www.usembassy.org.uk).

LOST AND FOUND

● To report lost credit cards:
American Express
☎ 800/528-2121;
Diners Club/Carte Blanche
☎ 800/234-6377;
MasterCard
☎ 800/826-2181;
Visa ☎ 800/227-6811
● Lost traveler's checks:
American Express
☎ 800/221-7282;
Thomas Cook
☎ 800/223-7373

PARKING

If you plan on driving in Boston, note that the city is notorious for its lack of parking. That said, follow these tips, and you should do fine:
● Look for public parking garages. Though more costly, these are by far the most convenient, as they are plentiful (especially Downtown). The garage under the Common is the most economical at $25 for 24 hours, $6 for additional hours.
● Allow extra time. Some destinations have garages and/or valet, some don't. If the latter, circle until you get lucky enough to find an empty spot on the street. Look for side streets but be careful not to park in "residents only" streets (which include most).
● Pay attention to parking signs on the street. Boston's meter maids are merciless.

STUDENT TRAVELERS

● To get discounts on the T and admissions, get an International Student Identity Card (ISIC). If you are not a student but are under 26, get the International Youth Card (IYC).
● The Council on International Educational Exchange (CIEE) has a Travel Service offering domestic air passes for bargain travel within the US. It is also the exclusive agent for several student-discount cards.
✉ 273 Newbury Street, Boston, MA 02116 ☎ 617/266-1926).
● Members of the Youth Hostel Association of England and Wales (✉ Trevelyan House, 8 St. Stephen's Hill, St. Albans, Herts, AL1 2DY ☎ 01727 855215) can use youth hostels.
● Information on student hostels within the US can be obtained from Hostelling International–American Youth Hostels
✉ 1105 Commonwealth Avenue, Boston, MA 02215 ☎ 617/779-0900; fax 617/779-0904; email: admin_hienec@usahostels.org; www.usahostels.org

TELEPHONES

● The area code for Boston and Cambridge is 617. This must be included even when making local calls. Some communities outside the city have different area codes.
● To call the US from the UK dial 00 1, followed by the area code and the number.
● To call the UK from the US, dial 011 44, then drop the initial zero from the area code.

TICKETS

● The one-year Boston CityPass (adult $39.50; seniors and children ages 3–11 $21.25) gives free admission for one visit each at six key sights: the Museum of Fine Arts (▷ 70–71), the Museum of Science (▷ 28–29), the New England Aquarium (▷ 53), the John F. Kennedy Library and Museum (▷ 103), Harvard Museum of Natural History (▷ 89) and Prudential Skywalk (▷ 73). Available from the above or at the visitor information center on Boston Common (▷ 50), in the Prudential Center (▷ 73) or on their website www.citypass.com/city/boston.

TOURIST OFFICES
● **Greater Boston Convention & Visitors Bureau Inc.** ✉ 2 Copley Place, Suite 105, Boston, MA 02116 ☎ 617/ 536-4100; fax 617/424-7664; www.bostonusa.com
● **Massachusetts Office of Travel & Tourism** ✉ State Transportation Building, 10 Park Plaza, Suite 4510, Boston, MA 02116 ☎ 617/973-8500; fax 617/973-8525; www.massvacation.com
● **Boston National Historical Park Visitor Center** ✉ 15 State Street, opposite Old State House ☎ 617/242-5642
● **Boston Common Information Kiosk** ✉ 147 Tremont Street ☎ 617/426-3115
● **Cambridge Office for Tourism** ✉ 4 Brattle Street, Harvard Square, Cambridge ☎ 617/441-2884

STAYING WIRED
Hopping on the internet is increasingly easy in Boston; many cafés in Back Bay (particularly on Newbury Street) offer free wireless services, as do many shops and salons in the Back Bay area. The Boston Public Library also has free wireless internet access and the entire downtown Salem has Wi-Fi.

EMERGENCY MEDICAL TREATMENT

Ambulance, fire, police	☎ 911
Massachusetts General Hospital	☎ 617/726-2000
Inn-House Doctor	☎ 617/859-1776 ⏰ 24 hours. Makes hotel visits
Late night pharmacies: CVS	✉ Porter Square (35 White Street, near Massachusetts Avenue), Cambridge ☎ 617/876-5519 ⏰ 24 hours ✉ 155 Charles Street, Boston ☎ 617/523-1028 ⏰ Mon–Fri 7am–midnight, Sat, Sun 9–9
Dental emergency	☎ 617/636-6828
Eye and Ear Infirmary	☎ 617/523-7900
Physician Referral Service	☎ 617/726-5800 ⏰ Mon–Fri 8.30–4.45

CONSULATES

Canada	✉ 3 Copley Place ☎ 617/262-3760
Great Britain	✉ One Memorial Drive, Cambridge ☎ 617/245-4500
Ireland	✉ 535 Boylston Street ☎ 617/267-9330
Italy	✉ 100 Boylston Street ☎ 617/542-0483
Portugal	✉ 699 Boylston Street ☎ 617/536-8740
Spain	✉ 545 Boylston Street ☎ 617/536-2506

Timeline

NEED TO KNOW TIMELINE

REVOLUTION

In the 1760s Britain imposed taxes on her New England colonists. Increasingly angry at interference in their lucrative seafaring trade, the colonists, led by Sons of Freedom Sam Adams and John Hancock, protested at having to pay taxes when they had no representation in the government that was taxing them. Tension began to mount and on March 5, 1770 British soldiers killed five colonists in what became known as the Boston Massacre. On December 16, 1773, Patriots protested against the Tea Act by throwing tea into the sea (the Boston Tea Party). British retaliation made war inevitable.

From left: American Revolution reenactment; statue of a Minute Man on the spot where events sparked the revolution; plaque on the grave of Samuel Adams; equestrian statue of Paul Revere; obelisk commemorating the Battle of Bunker Hill

Pre-1620 The Algonquins inhabit the Boston area.

1620 Pilgrims arrive on the *Mayflower* and establish the first English colony in Plymouth.

1629 Puritans found the Massachusetts Bay Colony in Charlestown.

1630 The colony moves to Beacon Hill on the Shawmut Peninsula.

1636 Harvard College is founded.

1680 Most of Boston is concentrated in what is to become the North End, around the flourishing seaport.

1775 The Revolution starts in Boston.

1776 The British leave Boston on March 17. On July 18, the Declaration of Independence is read from the State House balcony.

1790s Trade with China brings prosperity.

1795 Architect Charles Bulfinch starts the new State House. Five years later he helps to develop Beacon Hill.

1826 Mayor Josiah Quincy extends the waterfront and builds Quincy Market.

1840s Irish immigrants, fleeing the Potato Famine, pour into the North End.

1856 Work begins on filling in and developing the Back Bay as a new residential area.

1877 Swan Boats—distinctive boats with large model swans at the helm—come to the Public Garden.

1897 The Boston marathon is launched.

1918 The Red Sox win baseball's World Series—their first pennant victory. Their next victory was not to be until 2004.

1960s–70s An extensive urban renewal scheme includes John Hancock Tower.

1990 The US's biggest art theft occurs at the Isabella Stewart Gardner Museum.

1995 FleetCenter replaces the Boston Garden, home of the Bruins (ice hockey) and Celtics (basketball).

2004 New England Patriots win the Super Bowl for the second time since 2002. The Boston Red Sox win the World Series championship for the first time in almost a century.

2006 The Big Dig, Boston's decade-long, large-scale construction project to ease Boston's huge traffic problem, finally ends.

2007 Institute of Contemporary Art opens as part of revitalization of Boston's waterfront. Red Sox win the World Series again.

PAUL REVERE'S RIDE

In his lifetime Paul Revere (1735–1818) was known as a silversmith, but he was immortalized—with some poetic license—as a hero of the Revolution by the poet Henry Wadsworth Longfellow. Revere was a messenger for the Sons of Liberty and on the eve of the first battle of the Revolution rode to Lexington to warn local militia men about British preparations.

JFK

John Fitzgerald Kennedy was born in the Boston suburb of Brookline in 1917. His grandfather, "Honey-Fitz," was one of a long line of Irish mayors. Kennedy was elected president in 1960—good-looking and charismatic, he was a symbol of the nation's hope for a progressive future. He was assassinated on November 22, 1963.

Index

Boston's
25 BEST

WRITTEN BY Sue Gordon
ADDITIONAL WRITING Alexandra Hall and Michael Blanding
DESIGN WORK Jacqueline Bailey
COVER DESIGN Tigist Getachew
INDEXER Marie Lorimer
IMAGE RETOUCHING AND REPRO Michael Moody, Sarah Montgomery
REVIEWING EDITOR Paul Eisenberg

UPDATED BY Barbara Rogers

ISBN 978-1-4000-0796-7

SIXTH EDITION

IMPORTANT TIP
Time inevitably brings changes, so always confirm prices, travel facts, and other perishable information when it matters. Although Fodor's cannot accept responsibility for errors, you can use this guide in the confidence that we have taken every care to ensure its accuracy.

SPECIAL SALES
This book is available for special discounts for bulk purchases for sales promotions or premiums. Special editions, including personalized covers, excerpts of existing books, and corporate imprints, can be created in large quantities for special needs. For more information, write to Special Markets/Premium Sales, 1745 Broadway, MD 6–2, New York, NY 10019 or email specialmarkets@randomhouse.com.

Color separation by Keenes, Andover, UK
Printed and bound by Leo Paper Products, China
10 9 8 7 6 5 4 3 2 1

The Automobile Association wishes
picture libraries for their assistance i

Abbreviations for the picture credits
centre; (AA) AA World Travel Librar

1 AA/J Nicholson; **2** AA/M Lynch; **3**
Lynch; **5c** AA/C Sawyer; **6t** AA/M L
6bl AA/C Sawyer; **6bcl** AA/C Saw
AA/J Nicholson; **7cr** AA/C Sawyer
AA/M Lynch; **9** AA/M Lynch; **10t** A
AA/C Coe; **10/11b** AA/C Coe; **11**
AA/M Lynch; **13t** AA/M Lynch; **13**
13cb Brand X Pictures; **13b** AA/M
Sawyer; **14cb** AA/C Sawyer; **14b**
AA/M Lynch; **16ct** AA/M Lynch;
17t AA/M Lynch; **17ct** AA/C Saw
18t AA/M Lynch; **18ct** AA/C Saw
Kenward; **19t** AA/J Nicholson;
AA/C Sawyer; **20/21** AA/C Saw
24/25t AA/C Coe; **24/25c** AA/
Nicholson; **27l** AA/C Sawyer; **2**
AA/C Sawyer; **29tr** Museum o
AA/C Sawyer; **30** AA/J Nichol
33r AA/M Lynch; **34l** AA/J Ni
35r AA/C Coe; **36** AA/C Coe;
37r AA/J Nicholson; **38t** AA/
38br A/C Sawyer; **39t** AA/C
American History; **40** AA/J N
44 AA/C Coe; **45** AA/C Saw
Swerve/Alamy; **51r** © Swer
Scofidio + Renfro Architect
Contemporary Art/Boston,
53l AA/C Sawyer; **53r** AA/
55b AA/C Sawyer; **56t** AA
AA/J Nicholson; **58** AA/S
62 Bananastock; **63** AA/C
AA/C Coe; **68/69** AA/J Ni
Sawyer; **72l** AA/C Sawyer
Nicholson; **74/75** AA/J N
78t AA/C Sawyer; **78b** A
82 Photodisc; **83** Digital
AA/C Sawyer; **89r** AA/C
AA/C Coe; **91cl** AA/C Sa
AA/J Nicholson; **93** AA/
97t Photodisc; **97c** AA/
Neelon/Alamy; **103l** Ke
AA/C Sawyer; **104b** AA
106bcl AA/C Coe; **106**
Sawyer; **108t** AA/C Sa
108b AA/C Sawyer; **1**
Sawyer; **113** AA/C Sa
118 AA/C Coe; **119** A
Currency; **121t** AA/C
124bl AA/J Lynch; **12**
Sawyer; **125br** AA/C

Every effort has bee
any unintentional o
following edition o

A03615
Maps in this title produced from mapping © MAIRDUMONT / Falk Verlag 2009
Transport map © Communicarta Ltd, UK

Boston's
25 BEST

WRITTEN BY Sue Gordon
ADDITIONAL WRITING Alexandra Hall and Michael Blanding
DESIGN WORK Jacqueline Bailey
COVER DESIGN Tigist Getachew
INDEXER Marie Lorimer
IMAGE RETOUCHING AND REPRO Michael Moody, Sarah Montgomery
REVIEWING EDITOR Paul Eisenberg

UPDATED BY Barbara Rogers

ISBN 978-1-4000-0796-7

SIXTH EDITION

IMPORTANT TIP
Time inevitably brings changes, so always confirm prices, travel facts, and other perishable information when it matters. Although Fodor's cannot accept responsibility for errors, you can use this guide in the confidence that we have taken every care to ensure its accuracy.

SPECIAL SALES
This book is available for special discounts for bulk purchases for sales promotions or premiums. Special editions, including personalized covers, excerpts of existing books, and corporate imprints, can be created in large quantities for special needs. For more information, write to Special Markets/Premium Sales, 1745 Broadway, MD 6–2, New York, NY 10019 or email specialmarkets@randomhouse.com.

Color separation by Keenes, Andover, UK
Printed and bound by Leo Paper Products, China
10 9 8 7 6 5 4 3 2 1

A03615
Maps in this title produced from mapping © MAIRDUMONT / Falk Verlag 2009
Transport map © Communicarta Ltd, UK

The Automobile Association wishes to thank the following photographers, companies and picture libraries for their assistance in the preparation of this book.

Abbreviations for the picture credits are as follows – (t) top; (b) bottom; (l) left; (r) right; (c) centre; (AA) AA World Travel Library.

1 AA/J Nicholson; 2 AA/M Lynch; 3 AA/M Lynch; 4t AA/M Lynch; 4c AA/M Lynch; 5t AA/M Lynch; 5c AA/C Sawyer; 6t AA/M Lynch; 6cl AA/C Sawyer; 6c AA/M Lynch; 6cr AA/M Lynch; 6bl AA/C Sawyer; 6bcl AA/C Sawyer; 6bcr AA/C Coe; 6br Photodisc; 7t AA/M Lynch; 7cl AA/J Nicholson; 7cr AA/C Sawyer; 7bl AA/M Lynch; 7bc AA/J Nicholson; 7br AA/M Lynch; 8 AA/M Lynch; 9 AA/M Lynch; 10t AA/M Lynch; 10ct AA/M Lynch; 10c AA/C Sawyer; 10/11cb AA/C Coe; 10/11b AA/C Coe; 11t AA/M Lynch; 11ct AA/M Lynch; 11c AA/C Sawyer; 12 AA/M Lynch; 13t AA/M Lynch; 13tct AA/C Sawyer; 13ct AA/J Nicholson; 13c AA/J Nicholson; 13cb Brand X Pictures; 13b AA/M Lynch; 14t AA/M Lynch; 14ct AA/C Sawyer; 14c AA/C Sawyer; 14cb AA/C Sawyer; 14b AA/C Sawyer; 15t AA/M Lynch; 15b AA/C Sawyer; 16t AA/M Lynch; 16ct AA/M Lynch; 16c AA/C Sawyer; 16cb AA/C Sawyer; 16b AA/J Nicholson; 17t AA/M Lynch; 17ct AA/C Sawyer; 17c AA/M Lynch; 17cb AA/C Sawyer; 17b AA/C Sawyer; 18t AA/M Lynch; 18ct AA/C Sawyer; 18c AA/J Nicholson; 18cb AA/C Sawyer; 18b AA/P Kenward; 19t AA/J Nicholson; 19ct AA/C Sawyer; 19c AA/J Nicholson; 19cb AA/C Coe; 19b AA/C Sawyer; 20/21 AA/C Sawyer; 24tl AA/C Sawyer; 24cl AA/C Sawyer; 24cr AA/C Sawyer; 24/25t AA/C Coe; 24/25c AA/C Coe; 25r AA/J Nicholson; 26l AA/C Sawyer; 26r AA/J Nicholson; 27l AA/C Sawyer; 27r AA/C Sawyer; 28l AA/C Sawyer; 28r AA/C Sawyer; 28/9 AA/C Sawyer; 29tr Museum of Science, Boston; 29cl Museum of Science, Boston; 29cr AA/C Sawyer; 30 AA/J Nicholson; 30/1 AA/C Sawyer; 32l AA/C Sawyer; 32/3 AA/C Sawyer; 33r AA/M Lynch; 34l AA/J Nicholson; 34c AA/C Sawyer; 34r AA/C Coe; 35l AA/J Nicholson; 35r AA/C Coe; 36 AA/C Coe; 36/37t AA/C Sawyer; 36/37b AA/J Nicholson; 37l AA/C Coe; 37r AA/J Nicholson; 38t AA/C Sawyer; 38bl Greater Boston Convention & Visitors Bureau; 38br A/C Sawyer; 39t AA/C Sawyer; 39bl AA/J Nicholson; 39br Museum of African American History; 40 AA/J Nicholson; 41 AA/C Sawyer; 42 AA/C Sawyer; 43 Digital Vision; 44 AA/C Coe; 45 AA/C Sawyer; 46 AA/C Sawyer; 47 AA/C Sawyer; 50 AA/M Lynch; 51l © Swerve/Alamy; 51r © Swerve/Alamy; 52l The Institute of Contemporary Art/Boston, Diller Scofidio + Renfro Architects, Photo: (c) Iwan Baan; 52r Founders' Gallery, The Institute of Contemporary Art/Boston, Diller Scofidio + Renfro Architects, Photo: Peter Vanderwarker; 53l AA/C Sawyer; 53r AA/C Sawyer; 54t AA/C Sawyer; 54b AA/C Sawyer; 55t AA/C Sawyer; 55b AA/C Sawyer; 56t AA/C Sawyer; 56bl Old South Meeting House; 56br AA/C Sawyer; 57 AA/J Nicholson; 58 AA/S McBride; 59 Digital Vision; 60 Brand X Pictures; 61 AA/P Bennett; 62 Bananastock; 63 AA/C Coe; 66l AA/C Sawyer; 66r AA/C Sawyer; 67l AA/C Sawyer; 67t AA/C Coe; 68/69 AA/J Nicholson; 69 AA/J Nicholson; 70 AA/J Nicholson; 70/71 AA/C Sawyer; 72l AA/C Sawyer; 72r AA/C Sawyer; 73l AA/J Nicholson; 73r AA/C Sawyer; 74 AA/J Nicholson; 74/75 AA/J Nicholson; 76 AA/M Lynch; 76/77 AA/C Sawyer; 77 AA/C Sawyer; 78t AA/C Sawyer; 78b AA/M Lynch; 79 AA/J Nicholson; 80 AA/C Sawyer; 81 AA/C Sawyer; 82 Photodisc; 83 Digital Vision; 84 Brand X Pictures; 85 AA/C Coe; 88 AA/C Sawyer; 89l AA/C Sawyer; 89r AA/C Sawyer; 90l AA/M Lynch; 90tr AA/M Lynch; 90/91 AA/M Lynch; 91t AA/C Coe; 91cl AA/C Sawyer; 91cr AA/M Lynch; 92t AA/C Sawyer; 92bl AA/M Lynch; 92br AA/J Nicholson; 93 AA/J Nicholson; 94 AA/J A Tims; 95 AA/C Sawyer; 96 Brand X Pictures; 97t Photodisc; 97c AA/D Corrance; 98 AA/T Souter; 99 AA/M Lynch; 102 ©Michael Neelon/Alamy; 103l Kennedy Presidential Library; 103r Kennedy Presidential Library; 104t AA/C Sawyer; 104b AA/C Sawyer; 105 AA/P Bennett; 106t AA/P Bennett; 106bl AA/J Lynch; 106bcl AA/C Coe; 106bc AA/C Coe; 106bcr AA/C Sawyer; 106br AA/J Lynch; 107 AA/C Sawyer; 108t AA/C Sawyer; 108ct AA/M Lynch; 108c AA/C Sawyer; 108cb AA/S McBride; 108b AA/C Sawyer; 109 AA/C Sawyer; 110 AA/C Sawyer; 111 AA/C Sawyer; 112 AA/C Sawyer; 113 AA/C Sawyer; 114 AA/C Coe; 115 AA/C Coe; 116 AA/C Coe; 117 AA/C Coe; 118 AA/C Coe; 119 AA/C Coe; 120t AA/C Coe; 120b MRI Bankers' Guide to Foreign Currency; 121t AA/C Coe; 121b AA/M Lynch; 122 AA/C Coe; 123 AA/C Coe; 124t AA/C Coe; 124bl AA/J Lynch; 124br AA/C Sawyer; 125t AA/C Coe; 125bl AA/C Coe; 125bc AA/C Sawyer; 125br AA/C Sawyer.

Every effort has been made to trace the copyright holders, and we apologise in advance for any unintentional omissions or errors. We would be pleased to apply any corrections in any following edition of this publication.